WWII Gold Star Veterans of Wyoming County, New York

WWII SERVICE MEMBERS WHO MADE
THE SUPREME SACRIFICE

James Gillen

Wyoming County Historian's Office
WARSAW, NEW YORK

Published by the Wyoming County Historian's Office
26 Linwood Avenue
Warsaw, New York 14569

Copyright © 2019 by Wyoming County Historian's Office.
All rights reserved.

WWII Gold Star Veterans of Wyoming County, New York/
James Gillen. —1st ed.
ISBN 978-0-9997788-0-7

Library of Congress Control Number: 2019919141

Front Cover Image: *Richard Albert Rowe*, Middlebury.
Back Cover Image: *Normandy, France Sept. 1945.* Taken by Nick Devolos. Used with permission from his son, George Devolos.

No part of this publication may be reproduced, distributed or transmitted in any form or by any means, including photocopying, recording, or other electronic or mechanical methods, without the prior written permission of the publisher, except in the case of brief quotations embodied in critical reviews and certain other noncommercial uses permitted by copyright law. For permission requests, write to the publisher.

Contents

Gold Star List 1

Arcade 5

Attica 9

Bennington 37

Castile 41

Covington 49

Eagle 53

Gainesville 59

Genesee Falls 73

Java 77

Middlebury 79

Orangeville 85

Perry 87

Pike 111

Sheldon 117

Warsaw 121

Wethersfield 143

Attributed to Wyoming 145

Acknowledgements 149

Index 151

There's a gold star in our window
For a boy who was one of the best
But God called him up to Glory
For a well-earned and needed rest
Someday we'll understand
Why our silver star turned to gold
When we all meet up in glory
And our dear boys face we behold.

~ Author Unknown ~

In Memoriam

When war came on December 7, 1941, the sons and daughters of Wyoming County, New York answered their country's call without hesitation and manned the ramparts which were being threatened by a powerful enemy.

From shop and school, from hamlet and village, from farm and factory, they rallied to the flag for which their fathers and their fathers' fathers had fought.

In common with the rest of our peace loving country, however, few of them were prepared in the ordinary military sense for the gigantic struggle ahead. The manual of arms, the Articles of War, and the complexity of modern weapons, for most were heretofore unexplained mysteries, to be fathomed in faraway training camps and on the bloody battlefields of the world.

But what they lacked in military preparedness they made up in moral preparedness, in the far more important conviction, born at Bunker Hill and in Independence Hall and in the speeches of Patrick Henry and never lost, that no price was too dear to pay for liberty, even life itself.

Many Wyoming County service men paid the price. Following is the roll of sacrifice. It should serve also as a scroll of remembrance that we who are alive and free today by virtue of their sacrifices may never forget the sacred trust imposed upon us by their death.

(Used with permission obtained by the author from the Buffalo Evening News. Wyoming replaces original word Erie.)

CHAPTER ONE

Gold Star List

WYOMING COUNTY, NEW YORK SERVICE MEMBERS WHO MADE THE SUPREME SACRIFICE.

World War II

December 7, 1941 to September 2, 1945

Robert R. Allen	Attica	Navy
William H. Atwell	Warsaw	Army
Jesse C. Ballard	Eagle	Army
George W. Banks Jr.	Attica	Army
Frank Barnes	Warsaw	Navy
Ernest L. Bauer	Warsaw	Army Air Forces
Elmer J. Boatfield	Castile	Army
Robert J. Boatfield	Covington	Army Air Forces
Harold Q. Bostian	Middlebury	Army
William H. Browne	Warsaw	Army
Charles R. Burgett	Perry	Army Air Forces
Charles L. Campbell	Attica	Army
Charles R. Cannon	Bennington	Army
James F. Conway	Attica	Army Air Forces

John A. Coons	Attica	Cadet Air Corps
Edward J. Courtney	Gainesville	Marine Corps
Casimer J. Czerminski	Castile	Navy
Kermit A. Davis	Castile	Army
Willard T. DeGolyer	Castile	Army Air Corps
Rodney O. DeMun	Perry	Army
Alexander Dubovy	Warsaw	Army
Alton E. Dukelow	Perry	Army
Robert C. Dumbleton	Gainesville	Army Air Forces
Richard K. Eichenberger	Attica	Army
Leonard E. Emery	Perry	Army
George E. Ernst	Attica	Navy
Edward V. Fenner	Warsaw	Army
William S. Field	Middlebury	Army
Norman J. Fix	Attica	Army Air Forces
James Gell	Gainesville	Army
Bertrand C. George	Attica	Army
Leon W. George	Sheldon	Army
Kenneth J. Glor	Attica	Army
Robert K. Gracey	Attica	Navy
Harry W. Gumaer Jr.	Warsaw	Army Air Forces
Edward R. Hall	Perry	Army
Robert J. Hess	Eagle	Army
Ward S. Hewitt	Perry	Army
George M. Hickey	Castile	Army
John W. Holmes	Castile	Army
Theodore W. Hunt	Pike	Marine Corps
Paul C. Husted	Gainesville	Army Air Forces
Stephen S. Jackson	Attica	Army
William H. Judd	Perry	Army
Warren G. Kader	Eagle	Army

Joseph R. Knack	Perry	Army
William N. Knight	Warsaw	Army
Raymond Kolacinski	Perry	Marine Corps
Alfred S. Kosciolek	Perry	Army Air Forces
Harold R. Kuppinger	Attica	Army
Richard F. Laird	Sheldon	Navy
Leon E. Lathrop	Genesee Falls	Marine Corps
Robert S. Lathrop	Genesee Falls	Army Air Corps
Donald W. (Redden) Lauer	Arcade	Coast Guard
Maurice T. Lester	Warsaw	Navy
Francis B. Lippold	Attica	Navy
John E. Maher	Sheldon	Marine Corps
Bennie (Benny) P. Marino	Perry	Army
Wilson F. Marzolf	Warsaw	Army
Robert E. Mayhew	Perry	Army
Jack McGee	Covington	Army
Horatio R. Migliore	Perry	Army
Melvin O. Miller	Warsaw	Army
Martin H. Mulner Jr.	Attica	Army Air Forces
Donald E. Myers	Attica	Army
Basil Numack	Gainesville	Army Air Forces
Thomas P. O'Brien	Gainesville	Army
Thomas A. Parker Jr.	Perry	Army
John F. Phelan	Attica	Navy
Donald M. Prentice	Perry	Army Air Forces
Bernard O. Reding	Attica	Marine Corps
Evan H. Rice	Arcade	Army Air Forces
Lawrence E. Rider	Perry	Army Air Forces
Laverne P. Rissinger	Eagle	Army Air Forces
Floyd K. Roberts	Eagle	Army
Richard A. Rowe	Middlebury	Army Air Forces

John A. Schadt	Middlebury	Army
Henry P. Schell	Gainesville	Army
John F. Schwab	Warsaw	Army
James W. Scott	Warsaw	Army
Walter W. Shearing	Gainesville	Army
John H. Smith	Gainesville	Army
William A. Snyder	Arcade	Army
Richard N. Spellicy	Perry	Army
Donald H. Spencer	Attica	Navy
Merrill T. Spring	Castile	Army Air Forces
Duane W. Stevens	Warsaw	Army Air Forces
Grant G. Stout	Pike	Army Air Forces
Eugene N. Straub	Attica	Navy
Robert H. Summers	Bennington	Army
Michael Surtel	Perry	Army
Anthony J. Tortorice Jr.	Perry	Army
Herbert C. Trace	Perry	Army
Glenn E. VanValkenburg	Arcade	Navy
Theodore E. Wagner	Gainesville	Army
David D. Wallace	Warsaw	Army Air Forces
Maurice B. Walsh Jr.	Attica	Marine Corps
Frank R. Whaley	Attica	Army
Walter J. Wilcox Jr.	Warsaw	Army
James L. Woodley	Warsaw	Navy
Gordon K. Wright	Warsaw	Army
Eugene R. Youngberg	Pike	Navy
Francis A. Zahler Jr.	Attica	Army

CHAPTER TWO

Arcade

Donald William (Redden) Lauer

Chief Machinist Mate
U.S. Coast Guard

Donald William Redden Lauer was born October 9, 1915 in Arcade, NY, the son of William Redden and the former Adline Fledderman. His mother died on October 3, 1918. Donald was adopted by Mrs. Rose Lauer on December 15, 1919 and took the last name of Lauer.

In July of 1936 he enlisted in the U.S. Coast Guard at Buffalo, NY at the age of 20. He rose to the rank of Chief Petty Officer in six years. Donald had recently returned to Boston after assisting in building boats in DuLuth, MN. He had an honorable record in the service.

On November 28, 1942, he attended a popular nightclub called *The Cocoanut Grove*, along with approximately 1,000 other occupants, many of whom were people preparing to go overseas for military duty. A lit match used by an employee to change a light bulb, or possibly an electrical short, sparked a fire. Flammable decorations spread the fire rapidly and ultimately claimed 492 lives, including Donald's. Authorities estimated that approximately 300 of those killed could have been saved had the doors swung outward instead of inward and the capacity of the structure had not been exceeded.

He is buried in St. Peter and Paul Cemetery, Arcade, NY.

Survived by:
Parents: William Redden of Arcade and son of the late Adline Redden.
Adoptive Parent: Mrs. Rose Lauer of 138 E. Main Street, Arcade.
Brother: Urban Redden, US Air Force mechanic, stationed Amarillo, TX
Sister: Mrs. Rose (Redden) Davitt of Portland, OR.

Buffalo Evening News- December 2, 1942; December 3, 1942
Perry Herald, Perry, NY – December 4, 1942; December 11, 1942
*Birth Certificate
*Wyoming County Veterans Services Office

Evan Hayes Rice

2nd Lt., U.S. Army Air Forces

Evan Hayes Rice was born in 1916. He had worked as a supervisor in the Dunlop Tire and Rubber Company in Buffalo, NY. Evan was Arcade's first overseas casualty of World War II. Seven months before his death he married Eleanor Davis on December 25, 1942 while stationed at Avon Park, Florida.

Evan Rice entered the service from Buffalo on May 16, 1941. He received training as a cadet at Kelly Field, Gardner Field, and Pine Camp, NY; Fort Knox, Kentucky and Randolph Field in Texas. In October he was transferred to Lubbock Field in Texas. He was one of a class of 50 graduates at Lubbock Army Flying School. He obtained his pilots wings on Dec. 13, 1942, along with the rank of 2nd Lt., serving with the 319 AAF Bomb Group.

After graduation he was transferred to the Bomber Group at Avon Park. He left for overseas March 17, 1943. On July 11th the same year, in a raid on Gerbino Landing Ground No. 13 Sicily, his B-26 bomber which he co-piloted did not return from a mission. It was reported that the plane had been forced down in unfriendly territory over Sicily, Italy. He was 27. The War Department reported, "The plane had encountered enemy fire and was shot down. It was reported that possibly they may have been taken prisoner." However, the plane had crashed and all were killed.

He was buried in the temporary cemetery GELA on Sicily October 3, 1943 and later brought back to be buried in Arcade Rural Cemetery, Arcade, New York.

Decorations: Gold Cross, Purple Heart, European-African Campaign Medal.

Survived by:
Wife: Eleanor Davis Rice of Black Creek, NY.
Parents: Blaine A. and Elsie Rice of 129 North St. in Arcade.
Sister: Mrs. Pauline Hally; Kittery, Boston, Massachusetts.
Brother: Cpl. Dudley Rice of Horseheads, serving in Iceland

*The Post, Ellicottville, NY – August 11, 1943
*The Perry Herald – August 6, 1943
*The Patriot and Free Press, Cuba, N.Y. – December 31, 1942

William Allison Snyder

Pvt., U.S. Army

Obituary: *Perry Herald* – October 24, 1941
"Private William A. Snyder, Fort Belvoir, Virginia who enlisted for service in the United States Army at Arcade, N.Y. six months ago, died Monday from injuries received in an automobile accident Sunday at the base hospital at Fort Belvoir. His only immediate survivor is his aunt, Mrs. Mary Woodmansee, of Olean. The body arrived on Tuesday and was removed to the Halwig Funeral parlor. His head stone in Mount View Cemetery, Olean, N.Y. reads William A. Snyder, 1904 – October 18, 1941, Inscription: Co I, 174th Infantry."

SEARCH YOUR CELLAR

You may be walking over a "gold mine" of junk. Old papers, rags, metal—all can be sold for salvage and converted to war needs. Read the Herald classified columns; they may help you dispose of scrap for a profit.

The Perry Herald—August 4, 1943

Glenn Ellsworth Van Valkenburg

Seaman 1st Class, U.S. Navy

Glenn Ellsworth Van Valkenburg was born in Buffalo, NY on September 13, 1925, although his parents were residents on Park Street in Arcade at the time. He attended Attica High School while living at Johnsonburg in Sheldon with his family.

He enlisted from Wyoming County on September 15, 1942, two days after his 17th birthday. The family resided at Varysburg, NY when Seaman Glenn first joined up. The family had then moved to 17 Liberty St. Batavia, NY shortly after Glenn enlisted.

He trained in Rhode Island, North Carolina and Virginia leaving for San Francisco, California to go overseas in January of 1944.

He was killed in action in the South Pacific area at the age of 19 on November 22, 1944. A telegram came only an hour after the father had received their last letter from him, saying that he was in good health.

His marker is in the National Memorial Cemetery of the Pacific in Honolulu, Hawaii, Plot N, Row O, Grave 761.

Survived by:
Parents: Gerald and Gladys Van Valkenburg of Batavia formerly from Arcade.
Brothers: Russell, at home; Jack Van Valkenburg, in India with the Air Transport Command.

*Western New Yorker – November 30, 1944
*Unknown paper dated December 22, 1944
*Daily News, Batavia, N.Y. – January 4, 1945
*National WWII Memorial

CHAPTER THREE

Attica

Roger Robert Allen

Pharmacist Mate, 1ˢᵗ Class
U.S. Navy

ROGER ALLEN
"Man should not be left alone."
Stunt Night (1-2-3); Treas. Soph.
Class; Vice-Pres. Science Club
(3); Junior Play Comm; Hallo-
we'en Dance Comm. (3); Dance
Orchestra (4).

Roger Robert Allen was born in Batavia, NY on December 25, 1922. The family moved to Attica where he graduated in 1940. A quote appearing next to his name in his senior yearbook, "Man should not be left alone," is appropriate for the soldier he would become. His family resided in Attica for several years before returning to Batavia. He attended Stratford Graduate School in Buffalo before entering the service. He was employed by the Niagara, Lockport and Ontario Power Company.

Roger enlisted on October 15, 1942 where he trained at the Great Lakes Naval Training Station. He was stationed in Los Angeles for more than a year before being assigned to detached duty with the Marines. On March 8, 1944 he married Donna M. Willey of Los Angeles and the next day left for training with Marine Corps at two different California bases. He went overseas in June of that year.

In action he wore the Marine uniform, and ashore he could wear either Navy or Marine uniform. Navy Medical Corpsmen go ashore with Marines in all engagements.

He served in the invasion of Peleliu Island, Pacific War Zone in the Palau Group when on October 6, 1944 he was reported missing, and later, killed in action. Word of his death arrived on the birthday of his sister Virginia. He was 21.

Survived by:
Wife: Donna (Willey) Allen of Los Angles, CA.
Parents: Robert H. and Marian (Perkins) Allen of Batavia, NY.
Sisters: Virginia, 17 and Marilyn, 16

Attica News – December 14, 1944
Rochester Times Union – December 12, 1944
Livingston Republican – December 14, 1944
The Torch, Attica High School Yearbook, 1940.

George William Banks Jr.

2nd *Lt.*

U.S. Army

George William Banks Jr. was born in Attica on December 26, 1924. His family lived on North Street and his father was employed at the Attica Mills. He graduated from Hamburg High School in June of 1942.

He left Hamburg, NY for Fort Niagara on March 3, 1943, and from there was sent to Camp White, Oregon with the 299th Combat Engineers. After serving in various camps he transferred to the Air Corps and attended the University of Denver as an Aviation Student preliminary to appointment as an Aviation Cadet. At Denver, he was named a squadron commander with the rank of captain at the 353rd College Training Detachment (Aircrew). Cancellation of the Air Cadet program returned him to his original outfit.

After his Ft. Belvoir commission, Lieut. Banks was assigned to the Aberdeen Proving Grounds Ordinance School and then went on to Ft. Lewis, Washington and Camp Beale, California for Pacific duty.

According to the *Hamburg Sun*, "En route to Luzon his transport was anchored at Pearl Harbor the night of V-J. Day. Describing the celebration Bill wrote: 'The fireworks reminded me of the Hamburg Fair.'"

Lt. Banks was with an army maintenance engineers unit processing heavy motorized equipment and other surplus goods. He had been overseas since August of 1945 serving with 739th Engineer Heavy Shop Company.

LT. GEORGE W. BANKS, JR.

A letter to his family dated April 8, 1946 told of the 200 Japanese prisoners and 50 Filipinos helping his unit handle the compressors, graders, tractors and scrapers that were being sold to the Philippines.

He died on April 18, 1946 of injuries sustained in a motor vehicle accident near Batangas, Luzon, Philippine Islands with burial at Manila American Cemetery and Memorial at Fort Bonifacio, Manila, Philippines, Plot D; Row 11; Grave 20.

Survived by:
Parents: Mr. and Mrs. George W. Banks, of Hamburg, (who would return to Wyoming County to the town of Castile by 1959).
Brother: James E. at home.
Sisters: Jeanne K. at home; Mrs. Martha Endress of Atlanta or Marietta, GA.

*Attica News –January 1, 1925; Unknown day, 1946
*Hamburg Sun, Hamburg, N.Y. – May 2, 1946
*Wyoming County Veterans Services Office
*National WWII Memorial

Charles Lowell Campbell

Pvt. 1st Class
U.S. Army

Charles Lowell Campbell was born on August 30, 1924 in Cory, PA. He graduated Attica High School in 1942. Under his caption in *The Torch* it reads: "Conspicuous by his absence." He was the son of the Rev. and Mrs. Charles C. Campbell, who was at the time Rector of St. Luke's Church in Attica, NY.

Charles enlisted in 1942 while enrolled at Hobart College and entered the army on June 9, 1943. His training was at Fort McClellan, Alabama and then transferred to US Air Service Transport Command at Point Auburn, AL.

He was sent overseas in October of 1944 where he served with distinction in the 19th Armored Infantry Battalion 14th Armored Division Reconnaissance Group at Camp Campbell, Kentucky.

On January 1, 1945 he was listed as missing in action. Eleven months later his parents were informed that he had been killed in action on January 1, 1945. At the time of his death, he was serving with a reconnaissance company of the 19th Armored Battalion with the Seventh Army near Baerenthal, France.

His original unmarked grave was found with a cross made of two sticks with an American Army helmet hung on it, near Frohnacker, Baerenthal, France. Later his body was moved to the National Cemetery at Saint Avold 25 miles from Metz, France along with 12,000 other American boys. He was brought back to the U.S. and buried in the Chautauqua Cemetery.

A report from the *Attica News* dated April 30, 1945 from Major General Edward F. Witsell, acting Adjutant General of the Army states, "Circumstances surrounding his disappearance now available in the War Department discloses that when last seen, your son was a driver for a lieutenant who had been assigned the mission of guiding the battalion vehicles from Riedheim and Imbsheim, France to Baerenthal, France. Enemy forces attacked and cut off Baerenthal from Mouterhouse, France, where the large portion of the battalion was located."

His name and war record became a part of a permanent National Roll of Honor established at Washington Cathedral in our nation's Capital for enshrinement in the War Memorial Chapel.

He was posthumously awarded the Purple Heart.

Survived by:
Parents: Rev. Charles C. and Estelle Campbell, Attica, NY
Sisters: Dorothy Ann Campbell, Attica, NY; Mrs. Jean Davis, Peoria, IL

The Torch, Attica High School yearbook – 1942

*Attica News – January 25, 1945; February 1, 1945; April 30, 1945; January 10, 1946; July 15, 1948

James F. Conway

Technical Sgt.
U.S. Army Air Forces

James F. Conway was born on April 30, 1922. After graduating from Attica High School, he attended Alfred University. He enlisted on December 27, 1941 in Buffalo, NY. James received his training at the following places: Jefferson Barracks, MO; Chanute Field, IL; Las Vegas, NV where he received his wings; Salt Lake City, UT; Ephrata, WA; Seattle, WA and Glasgow, MT.

He was sent to North Africa on February 21, 1943. He served with the 96th Bomber Squadron, 2nd Bomber Group.

In July 1943 while serving as a gunner on an airplane nicknamed "The Scrubby Old Goat," he was officially credited with shooting down four enemy planes over Sicily. His fellow crewmen then nicknamed Sgt. Conway "Fire Chief" for his accomplishments.

He had taken part in American attacks against the Axis in the African, Sicilian and Italian sectors. Early in July, he and other members of his Fortress crew were awarded special citations for downing seven of the twenty Axis planes which intercepted them in the invasion of Catania July 11th.

On August 27, 1943 while serving as turret gunner on a B-17 Flying Fortress, "The Cactus Clipper" he was reported missing when his plane crashed as a result of enemy anti-aircraft fire near Anzio, Italy.

In the crash, Conway and three others—being the co-pilot, waist gunner and tail gunner—were taken prisoner by the Germans. He was officially reported killed in action a year later on August 27, 1944. At the time of his death Sgt. Conway had completed 45 combat missions. The Air Medal, one Silver Oakleaf and three Bronze Oakleaf Clusters were presented to his mother, Mrs. James F. Conway in honor of her son.

James is buried in Italy in the Sicily-Rome American Cemetery and Memorial.

Survived by:
Parents: Mr. and Mrs. James F. Conway of 56 North Pearl Street.
Brother: Jack at home. He later went to Cornell University in Ithaca, NY.
Sisters: Joanne at home; Mrs. Jack Canty of Albany, NY; Mrs. Frances Kane and Mrs. Albert Rahn of 226 Bank Street and Mrs. Harry Watkins of 220 Washington Avenue all of Batavia, NY. (Two other sisters Dorothy and Jane died in infancy.)

Attica News – September 23, 1943; September 7, 1944
Western New Yorker – Jan. 18, 1945
The Torch, Attica High School yearbook, 1939.
*National WWII Memorial website

John A. Coons

Flying Cadet
Cadet Air Corps

John A. Coons was the son of Elizabeth and Arthur Coons. His parents divorced sometime before 1930. Elizabeth married Verne L. Shepard and they lived in Batavia for a time. John graduated from Batavia High School in 1935. In his senior year, John was a member of the National Honor Society, lettered in tennis, was in the school play and was the associated editor of "Pic". He was awarded a scholarship by DePauw University. His work at DePauw won him a scholarship for a year's study at Oslo, Norway, during his junior year. After high school the family moved to 300 Exchange Street in Attica. Upon John's graduating from DePauw in 1940 with high honors, he accepted a position as an assistant professor of Spanish on the faculty of the Wisconsin University up until his enlistment.

John's step-father, Vern L. Shepard, was serving in France during WWII. John himself enlisted in June of 1941 in the Flying Cadet Corps, but was not called to report until November 5th. At age 23 he completed the preliminary ground course at the Wilson Bonfils Flying School in Chickasha, Oklahoma. John had made his first solo flight just two weeks before he was killed when his airplane crashed during flight maneuvers near Chickasha on December 10, 1941.

Twenty Warsaw Minute Men from the Warsaw American Legion Post attended the funeral held at the home of County Commander Vern L. Shepard in Attica. Cadet Coons is buried there in Forest Hill Cemetery.

As part of WBTA's program dramatizing the lives of "Heroes of this War" the life history of Attica's first hero, Jack Coons was heard on the radio in April of 1944. Unfortunately, no known copy of it exists.

Survived by:
Father: Arthur Coons of Batavia.
Mother: Mrs. Vern L. Shepard of Attica.
Stepfather: Vern L. Shepard, also of Attica, would later become the Wyoming County Commander of the American Legion and the chef de guerre of the 40 & 8 Society.

*Western New Yorker – December 18, 1941
*Attica News - April 13, 1944

Richard Kenneth Eichenberger

Pvt. U.S. Army

Richard Kenneth Eichenberger was born on April 8, 1922 in Attica, NY. He attended Attica schools and graduated from South Byron High School. He was formerly from Attica but lived in South Byron, NY when he entered the service in October of 1944. He served with Co. D. 207th Infantry Training Battalion at Camp Blanding, Florida.

He was accidently killed during training maneuvers at Camp Blanding on January 21, 1945 at the age of 23. Burial was in Forest Hill Cemetery, Attica, NY.

Survived by:
Parents: Mr. and Mrs. Fred and Ruby Eichenberger of Attica.
Brothers: Robert Eichenberger at home; Sgt. Fred Eichenberger Jr. was in a hospital in Memphis with wounds to his left arm after being overseas.
Sister – Norma Jane at home.

*Attica News – April 8, 1922; January 25, 1945
*The Times, Batavia, NY. – January 25, 1945
*Rochester Times Union – Jan. 26, 1945
**Wyoming County Veterans Services Office

George Edward Ernst

Fire Controlman, 2nd Class
U.S. Navy

George Edward Ernst was born in Attica, NY on April 15, 1920. He graduated Attica High School and was on *The Torch* yearbook staff, Student Council, junior and senior play, Junior and Senior Ball Committee, Track Mgr. Vice President of the Senior Class and President of the Freshman Class. A quote from his senior yearbook read, "Join the navy and see the world."

He enlisted in the Navy in November of 1938 as an apprentice seaman. He trained at Naval Training Station at Newport, RI. In May of 1939 he was transferred to Norfolk VA, and in November, assigned to the *USS Sims*, a destroyer. He saw enemy action in 1942 in the epic naval battle, "The Battle of Coral Sea," where he survived the sinking of his ship. Returning to the United States, he had training in fire control work and range finding—learning how to aim and direct the guns of his ship.

He was assigned to the *USS Gansvoort* in August, 1942 and remained there until August of 1944 when he was stationed aboard the *USS Lindsey*. On April 12, 1945 near Mae Shima, southwest of Okinawa, he was killed aboard the *USS Lindsey* when a "minelayer"—two suicide planes one hitting on either side—cut the forward part of his ship away.

He was buried in Forest Hill Cemetery, Attica, New York.

Survived by:
Parents: George Anthony Ernst of Attica and the late Emma Foell Ernst.
Stepmother: Vera Urf Merle Ernst of Attica.
Sister: Mrs. Ethel (Charles) Kennedy.

Attica News – May 3, 1945; March 10, 1949
The Torch, Attica High School yearbook, 1938.
*Wyoming County Veterans Services Office

Norman J. Fix

Staff Sgt.
U.S. Army Air Forces

Norman J. Fix was born in Attica, NY, August 5, 1920 and was a 1939 graduate of Attica High School. He played baseball and intramural basketball. A quote from his senior yearbook under his name reads, "What is work and what have I to do with it?" He was employed as a mechanic before entering the Air Forces in December 1942.

Enlisting on July 28, 1942 at Buffalo, where he resided prior to the war, he then trained at Atlantic City, NJ, Redland, CA; Oregon, Walla Walla and Ephrata, WA; and Great Falls, MT before his bombardment group went overseas. Norman served as a Staff Sergeant and Ball Turret Gunner on B-17G with the US Army Air Forces, 615 Bomber Squadron, 401st Bomber Group.

On January 11, 1944, according to the War Department, the Eighth Air Force from its British bases carried out the heaviest attack of the war on German aircraft plants within 120 miles of Berlin at Oschersleben, Halberstadt and Brunswick. A total of 1200 American planes, including about 700 bombers, were said to have taken part.

A three hour aerial battle commenced with the Germans sending up every type of aircraft in a futile effort to keep the heavy bombers from their targets. Fifty-nine Fortresses and Liberators failed to return. German losses for the day were more than 152 fighter planes shot down by gun crews of the bombers and fighter planes which provided escort.

Sgt. Fix was one of the thousands of men lost in this one raid and was reported as missing in action but it was later determined that Norman and four other airmen were killed when his plane was attacked by German Aircraft causing the right wing to break off and crashed near Halberstadt, Germany. He was buried at Netherlands American Cemetery in Margraten, Netherlands in Block D, Row 8, Grave 18.

Survived by:
Parents: Albert and Viola Fix, 4 Genesee Street, Attica, NY.
Brothers: Alfred Fix, Frances W. Fix and Kenneth Fix who was serving in the European Mediterranean zone at the time of his brother's death.
Sister: Helen Fix, of Attica, NY.

*Attica News – January 27, 1944; March 30, 1944
*The Torch, Attica High School yearbook, 1939.
*Wyoming County Veterans Services Office
*National WWII Memorial website

Bertrand C. George

Sgt., U.S. Army

Bertrand C. George was born in Attica on October 28, 1917. He attended St. Vincent's Parochial School in Attica and graduated from Attica High School in 1938. During his high school years he was involved with the Scribbler Staff, Commercial Club, Dramatics Club, Glee Club, football and intramural basketball. A quote from a senior year book reads, "Just a mischievous chap but he means well." He was the third cousin of Lieut. Ed Don George. Bertrand was a former employee of the Chevrolet Motor and Axle plant in Buffalo. He was engaged to Miss Janet E. Dooley.

Upon entering the Army at Fort Niagara, NY on April 2, 1942 he found his place in the Quartermaster Corps. Sgt. George received his training at Fort McClellan, AL and Fort Dix, NJ. Bertrand also spent some time in Foreign Service at Churchill, Canada then returned to the US to become a member of the Transportation Corps at Camp Miles Standish, MA.

Sgt. George was sent overseas on March 3, 1943 with the Army Quarter Master Corp. He arrived in Oran, Algeria on March 5th and early in September was sent to Italy. His ship, the *USS Marshall*, was bombed during the Battle of Salerno and set afire while transferring supplies to small boats about 500 feet from the landing beach at Salerno, Italy. Only 40 men of the 200 plus crew members and officers were saved. Most of them were hospitalized for many months. Sgt. Bertrand C. George was killed in action in Italy on September 15, 1943 at the age of 25; the first of Attica's casualties. His remains were buried overseas and then brought back in 1948 to be buried at St. Vincent's Cemetery in Attica.

Survived by:
Parents: Sylvester and Mary Harman George, Village of Attica.
Brother: Gerald George of Buffalo, NY.

*Attica News – November 4, 1943
*Several unknown newspaper articles located at the Wyoming County Historian's Office.
*The Torch, Attica High School yearbook, 1938.
*Wyoming County Veterans Services Office

Kenneth J. Glor

Pvt. 1st Class
U.S. Army

Kenneth J. Glor was born in Attica on August 24, 1924. The Glor family had lived for many years on Exchange Street in the village of Attica, just below the Erie R.R. tracks, his father being a carpenter for the railroad. Kenneth was an Attica High School student and worked on farms in the area. He enlisted in the Army on his 18th birthday August 24, 1942 in Buffalo, NY.

Kenneth went overseas in October of 1942 and fought in North Africa during the Tunisian Campaign. He was captured and taken prisoner by the Germans. He later escaped and made his way back to allied lines. He then fought in the invasion of Sicily during the Sicilian Campaign. For several months he had served as acting sergeant.

On June 23, 1944 while fighting in France, he was killed in action at the age of 19. The body of Pfc. Kenneth J. Glor was brought back to the US in July of 1948 to be buried at the Lakeside Memorial Park Cemetery in Hamburg, NY.

Survived by:
Parents: George Glor and Alta Glor of 135 Lakeview Ave in Bayview, NY (Formerly of Attica.)
Brother: Ralph G. Glor, received a medical discharge from the Army while at Camp Gordon, FL.
Sisters: Mary, Mrs. Marvette Markivech, and Carol Glor all of Bennington.

Attica News – July 27, 1944; July 1948; August 3, 1944
Wyoming County Times – July 27, 1944
Buffalo Courier Express – July 22, 1944

Robert Kennedy Gracey

Fireman, 1ˢᵗ Class
U.S. Navy

Robert Kennedy Gracey was born on March 27, 1920. He went to Buffalo, along with two other young men, to enlist in February of 1938. He passed the examination and returned to complete his studies and graduate from Attica High School in June of the same year.

He was called to fulfill his enlistment on July 20, 1938. The others who had gone with him that day were turned down because they did not pass the physical, making Robert the first person from Attica to enlist for World War II.

Robert was a fireman on the tanker, *Neosho*. He became missing in action when the *Neosho* was sunk during the Navy's victory over the enemy during the Battle of Coral Sea, Pacific Theater on May 7, 1942.

In July of 1958, Robert's father, a former Marine and a guard at Attica Prison, approached the Director of Wyoming County Veteran's Services, Robert Kinglesy. Charles asked the Director to write a letter on his behalf to the Overseas Veterans Graves Division at Washington. Their initial telegram dated June 12, 1942 notifying them of their son's death stated if it wasn't possible  to send remains home, he would be "interred temporarily in the locality where the death occurred," was most likely standard wording. Over fourteen years had passed since Robert Gracey had been killed and the family had never been informed of it, nor told where he was buried. The request was forwarded to the Department of the Navy. No other paperwork in the file show any answer.

Robert Kennedy Gracey's body was never recovered when the *Neosho* sank during the Navy's battle for victory over the Japanese fleet. He is memorialized at Manila American Cemetery in Fort Bonifacio, Manila, Philippines and at the Battle of the Coral Sea Memorial Park in Queensland, Australia.

Survived by:
Parents: Charles & Bertha Gracey of 19 Elm St. in Attica.
Sisters: Naomi, at home; and Mrs. Juanita Wieczorek also of Attica.

Attica News – June 15, 1942; June 18, 1942
**The Torch*, Attica High School yearbook, 1938.
*National WWII Memorial website
*Wyoming County Veterans Services Office

Stephen S. Jackson

Pvt. 1st Class
U.S. Army

Stephen S. Jackson was born October 12, 1924 in Ossining, NY. He graduated Kingston High School in 1941. He moved with his mother to Attica in June of 1942. He entered the service at Ft. Niagara, NY on February 22, 1943 and went overseas in November, 1944. He was employed at the Genesee Street plant of the Curtiss-Wright Corporation.

Stephen was sent to the University of Illinois in Champagne for a college course in engineering under the army specialist program. Before entering the University, Private Jackson was with the Coast Artillery Anti-Aircraft at Fort Bliss, TX.

Pvt. Jackson served with the 53rd Armored Engineer Battalion, 8th Armored Division. He was riding in a half-track near Anrochte, Germany when his column came under fire. Stephen was killed by sniper fire April 5, 1945, during the Battle of the Ruhr (Ruhr Pocket). He was 21-years-old.

Initially he was buried in Margraten, Netherlands. On April 29, 1949 his body was met at the station in Kingston, NY by members of his family. Pvt. Jackson, under military escort, was taken to the funeral home of A. Carr & Sons and later reburied in Rosendale Plains Cemetery in Tillson, NY.

Survived by:
Parents: Viona S. Hennig and stepfather Clayton Hennig

Daily News, Batavia – July 24, 1943
The Citizen Register, Ossining, NY. – April 27, 1949
Kingston Daily Freeman, Kingston, NY. – April 29, 1949
*Wyoming County Veterans Services Office

Harold R. Kuppinger

Lt., U.S. Army

Harold R. Kuppinger was born in Attica where he received his first eight years of schooling and received the American Legion award in 8th grade before moving to Moravia, NY. In the 9th grade he received the American Legion award again. After graduating in 1934 as valedictorian of his class he entered Cornell University under a New York State tuition scholarship and a University undergraduate scholarship. He was the holder of the Knickerbocker Bursary. Harold was a honorary member of Eta Kappa Nu, the fraternity in electrical engineering and also of Pi Tau Pi Sigma, the fraternity of the Signal Corps. He graduated in 1938 and was employed by the New York Power & Light Co., at the time he entered the service on November 17, 1941. He had lived in Owasco, NY.

In addition to earning his degree, Harold received the commission of 2nd Lieutenant in the U. S. Army Reserve Corps by the president of the U.S. under the provisions of the National Defense Act upon the recommendation of President Edmund Day of Cornell University; and Col. Waldo C. Potter, professor of Military Science and tactics and the commandant of the R.O.T.C. unit, for completing the advanced course in the Reserve Officers Training Corps.

Lt. Kuppinger was first stationed in Florida and then took special training at Princeton University. He later served at Mitchel Field where he was assigned to an aircraft warning unit. Then, in March of 1942, he was sent to Puerto Rico and from there to the Pacific Theater.

On May 4, 1945, at the age of 27, he was killed in the invasion of Okinawa when the ship he was on was attacked by suicide dive bombers. He had been awaiting the trip to shore, where he was to have had a hand in the military governorship of the islands.

He was buried at Military Cemetery No. 3 Okinawa Island on May 5 1945. On July 8, 1949 he was brought back to the United States to be buried at Fort Hill Cemetery, Auburn, NY. He was posthumously awarded the Medal of Valor and the Purple Heart.

Survived by:
Wife: Evelyn Belding Kuppinger
Children: Kraig B., 3-years-old and Kurt Richard, 3-months-old
Parents: Mr. & Mrs. Henry Kuppinger of Owasco, NY.
Brothers: Henry L. and Blair F.

*Southern Cayuga Tribune – October 26, 1934
*Attica News – June 23, 1938; May 17, 1945; September 27, 1945
*Daily News, Batavia, NY. – October 2, 1945
*The Citizen Advertiser, Auburn, NY. – June 17, 1949
*Rochester Democrat and Chronicle – July 9, 1949

Francis Bernard Lippold

Yeoman 1st Class
U.S. Navy

Francis Bernard Lippold was born on May 6, 1907 in East Bennington, NY. He graduated from the Attica High School. He attended the Geneseo Normal School and Albany State Teachers College. A quote from his college yearbook read, "Real living makes the man." He had taught at Bayport High School in Bayport, Long Island and Wellington C. Mepham High School in Belmont, Long Island. He married Claire Genevieve Igoe on July 24, 1943 in New York City at the Church of St. Francis of Assisi.

He entered the service in July of 1942 and was stationed at Staten Island. He died on September 9, 1943 of leukemia at the U.S. Naval Hospital in Brooklyn, NY at the age of 36. He was buried at St. Vincent's Cemetery in Attica.

Survived by:
Wife: Clair Genevieve (Igoe) Lippold, North Brookfield, MA.
Parents: Mr. & Mrs. Joseph.Lippold, Darien Center, NY.
Brothers: Leo Lippold, at home; Edward Lippold and Clement Lippold both of Batavia, NY.
Sister: Mrs. John Maley, Batavia, NY.

Attica News – August 5, 1943; September 16, 1943
Pedagogue- New York State Teachers yearbook, 1932.

Martin H. Mulner Jr.

2nd Lt., U.S. Army Air Forces

Known as "Marty," Martin H. Mulner was born in 1921 at Batavia, NY. A former member of St. Joseph's Church and its fife and drum corps. He was a graduate of Attica High School. In the *Torch* senior yearbook from Attica, he was involved in basketball, tennis, track, Junior and Senior Play Committee, President of his Sophmore Class, and was part of the *Torch* staff. His quote for his yearbook read, "Activity is the only road to knowledge."

He entered the service in September 1943, going to Keesler Field for adaption and classification tests. Afterward he trained at San Antonio, then Brace Field, Ballinger, Goodfellow Field, San Angelo; and earning his wings at Foster Field, Victoria—all in Texas. At Foster Field he was commissioned second Lieutenant. He graduated as a fighter pilot and later trained with the speedy bombers before going into action. He reported to Randolph Field as one of the expert flyers selected for training in AAF Central Instructors School. Upon completion of a month's specialized training here, he went to another training field of the AAF Training Command as an instructor of aviation cadets.

After only a week at Independence, KA, a change in Army plans moved him and others to the Replacement Depot at Columbia, SC from which place he was assigned to the 345th Bombing Group, 498th Squadron and shipped to the Pacific Theater of operation. During his training he wrote a series of articles for the *Attica News*.

On May 26, 1945 he was listed as "missing in action" and it was later determined he was killed in action while piloting a B-25 bomber used in sweeps over Japanese-held territory over Formosa. His plane was struck by hidden anti-aircraft artillery just after deploying 250 pound parachute-retarded demolition bombs on the Kyoritsu Alcohol Refinery in Formosa. He was 24-years-old.

Lt. Mulner was buried in the National Memorial Cemetery of the Pacific in Honolulu, Hawaii.

Attica residents may recall that his parents owned and operated The Old Stage House Restaurant – (Hamilton) Hotel on Exchange Street in Attica.

Survived by:
Parents: Mr. and Mrs. Martin H. Mulner Sr., Attica, NY
Sisters: Mrs. Agnes Ray and Mrs. Mildred Ritchlin both of Batavia, NY; Mrs. Mary Godfrey of Williamsville, NY

*Attica News – August 31, 1944; June 14, 1945
*Daily News, Batavia – June 11, 1945
*The Torch, Attica High School yearbook, 1939.

Donald E. Myers

Pvt. 1st Class
U.S. Army

Donald E. Myers was born in Waterloo, NY on October 3, 1923. In 1935 his family moved to Attica, NY where Donald graduated from Attica High School. His senior achievements listed in the Attica yearbook, the *Torch* of 1941, were Business Manager of Eagle, Assistant Manager of *Torch*, Senior Benefit Committee. In the senior class chart of what will be, he stated, "Brass Button Man." His senior will reads, "I Don Myers, do will and bequeath my military uniform of the Astor Theater to Jack Turney."

He enlisted in the Army on August 16, 1943 and trained at Ft. McClellan, AL and Camp Pickett, VA before going overseas in October. He served with the 311th Infantry Regiment, 78th Infantry Division. He wrote a letter to his parents in Attica under the date of December 3, 1944 from Europe. On December 15, 1944 he was reported killed in action in Germany while serving with an infantry unit, he was 21-years-old. Donald didn't know that a week earlier, on December 7, his father Earl Myers had been killed in an auto accident in Depew, NY.

Pvt. Myers burial was at Henri-Chapelle American Cemetery, Belgium.

Survived by:
Parents: Ruth Gibbs of Waterloo, NY and the late Earl Myers of Attica.
Step-mother: Alberta R. Myers of Attica.
Sisters: Betty Myers, at home; Mrs. Gregory Brady of Batavia, NY.
Step-Brothers: Pvt. Russell Schriner in action in Italy; Stanley Schriner, California.
Step-Sister: Phyllis Myers, at home.

*Attica News – December 28, 1944
*Daily News, Batavia, NY. – December 27, 1944
*The Torch, Attica High School yearbook, 1938.
*National WWII Memorial

John F. Phelan

Aviation Radio Mechanic, 1st Class
U.S. Navy

John F. Phelan was born December 5, 1911 in New York City, the son of John and Alice Phelan. He came to Attica in November of 1938 from the Bronx to work at Attica State Prison.

Enlisting on July 6, 1942, he trained at Newport, RI; then Jacksonville and Hollywood, Florida; and was afterwards assigned to the aircraft carrier, *USS Bunker Hill*. He was home for a short furlough in February of 1945. His plane was lost in action in December 1945, somewhere in the Pacific. He had been serving as a radio operator on a dive bomber.

His name is on the Courts of the Missing, Honolulu Memorial in Hawaii.

Survived by:
Sister: Mary B. Phelan, Washington, DC.

Attica News – June 7, 1945; June 14, 1945

Bernard Otto Reding

Pvt., U.S. Marine Corps

Bernard Otto Reding was born August 21, 1924 in Batavia, NY. He attended St. Vincent's Roman Catholic School and Church in Attica and graduated from Attica High School.

He enlisted on June 9, 1944 and entered basic training at Parris Island. He was transferred for further training as a heavy machine gun operator to Camp Pendleton, Oceanside, California. From there he was shipped to the Pacific Theater on November 13, 1944 and received further training on Russell Island and at Guadalcanal with the 1st Division 7th Marines.

On May 18, 1945 he was instantly killed in action during the Battle of Okinawa Pacific Theater, at the age of 20. Only one man in his company escaped being wounded or killed. His body returned home February 16, 1949 by train for burial the next day in St. Vincent's Cemetery in Attica.

Survived by:
Parents: Elmo and Loretta (Petz) Reding of Attica.
Brothers: Robert at home; Edmund of Attica; Br. Cajeton of St. Joseph's Friary at Saranac Lake, NY; Paul at St. Joseph's Seminary in Callicoon, NY.
Sisters: Mary and Joan at home.

Attica News – June 7, 1945; February 17, 1949
The Torch, Attica High School yearbook, 1943.
*Wyoming County Veterans Services Office

Donald Houghton Spencer

Electricians Mate, 2ⁿᵈ Class
U.S. Navy

Donald Houghton Spencer was born November 2, 1921 in Akron, Ohio. A quote from him appeared in the Attica High School *Torch* yearbook reads, "The right man, in the right place, at the right time."

Donald tried to enlist in the Marines and the Navy in February of 1941 but, because of a dental deficiency, he was sent back home. After getting his teeth fixed he tried again, and on March 10, 1941 he was successful in joining the Navy in the Submarine Service.

His training was at the New London, CT Sub-base and attached to two different diving sections. He entered actual combat service in the Pacific theatre in January of 1943. Donald was a crewman aboard the

submarine *USS Grayling*, SS-209. The ship having not been heard from since August 20th he was reported missing in action in or near Tablas Strait, Philippine Islands on September 24, 1943.

In the *Attica Record* dated Jan. 17, 1946 an article from the Navy department to his parents states, "The war diary, Pacific Submarine Force, under date September 15, 1943 states that the Grayling was on route to Pearl Harbor from a port in the Southwest Pacific area. The Grayling failed to arrive at her destination and no further record of the submarine and her possible fate has ever been received by the Navy Department." All crewmen aboard the Grayling were officially declared deceased on January 3, 1946. He was posthumously awarded the Purple Heart.

Survived by:
Parents: Mr. and Mrs. Lawrence Spencer of 275 Main Street, Attica.

*Attica News – January 17, 1946
**Wyoming County Veterans Services Office
*The Torch- Attica High School yearbook, 1941.
*Note: More information on the Grayling can be found at www.oneternalpatrol.com/uss-grayling-209-loss.html

Eugene Neter Straub

Gunners Mate, 2nd Class
U.S. Navy

Eugene Neter Straub was born on March 29, 1919 in Darien Center, NY. He had enlisted twice. Eugene was honorably discharged in May of 1941 but re-enlisted in December to rejoin the fleet when war broke out. He was aboard the *USS Juneau,* a light cruiser, when it became engaged at Guadalcanal with the Japanese on November 13, 1942. After being struck by one torpedo it headed towards port for repairs when it was struck again, instantly sinking the ship. Approximately 115 survived the explosion but 687 others were killed. Only ten were recovered from the water when help arrived over a week later. Straub's family was notified by wire received on January 11, 1943, that Eugene was missing in action. His wife did not find out until later as she had already set out for San Francisco to spend a two week furlough with her husband.

A nephew, Andrew Straub of Warsaw, had one known picture of Eugene and kindly allowed us to use it for this book.  An interview with *The Batavia Daily News* dated April 2, 2018 was done with Andrew after the *USS Juneau* was recently discovered after 75 years, on March 17, 2018, 2.6 miles below the Pacific Ocean near the Solomon Islands.

Gunner Straub's name is memorialized at the Manila American Cemetery, Fort Bonifacio, Manila, Philippines and is recorded as died November 13, 1942. His daughter was born after he had left for service; he never got to see her.

Survived by:
Wife: Marion Emma Trick Straub of 12 Lauren Drive in Attica.
Daughter: Marjorie, 6-months-old at the time of Eugene's death.
Parents: Fred and Viola Straub of Darien Center, NY.

*Attica News – January 14, 1943
*The Daily News – Jan. 11, 1943; May 25, 1945; April 2, 2018 by Scott DeSmit
www.foxnews.com, March 20, 2018 by James Rogers
*www.smithsoian.com, March 22, 2018 by Jason Daley
*National WWII Memorial

Maurice Bernard Walsh Jr.

Lt., U.S. Marine Corps

Maurice Bernard Walsh was born on June 27, 1920 in Auburn, NY. He attended Batavia and Attica High Schools, graduating from the latter. In school he was involved in football, basketball, track, Glee Club, and was president of Sophomore Class, treasurer of Junior Class, and president of the Student Council. He was in the school operetta, the junior and senior play, was the president of the Dramatics Club, on the junior and senior Prom Committee, the *Torch* yearbook staff, and Junior Response. A quote about him in his yearbook was, "He's not merely a chip off the old block, but the block itself." His education was continued at Syracuse University and the New York College of Forestry.

He enlisted in the Marines on July 17, 1941 at Buffalo, NY. He trained at Parris Island, SC for basic military training where he was awarded marksman with riffle, automatic rifle, and pistol and received a sharp-shooter medal. Maurice was transferred to the Marine Guard Company, Jacksonville and afterwards transferred to Officers' Training School at Quantico, VA. He was a member of the 4th Marine Division.

On March 10, 1945 during the invasion of Iwo Jima, Pacific Theater he was seriously wounded in combat with a spinal injury. He was evacuated to the states but died in service on March 14, 1946 at the Oakland Naval Hospital at Oakland, CA. It was one year and four days after being wounded at the age of 25.

Lt. Walsh's body was laid to rest in St. Vincent's Cemetery in Attica.

Survived by:
Wife: Jane Cooper Walsh of Batavia, NY.
Child: Michael born June 1, 1945
Parents: Maurice B., Sr. and Julia E. Walsh 34 N. Pearl St. (formerly of 8 Hunt Blvd.) in Attica.

*Attica News – March 28, 1946
*Various newspaper clippings undated at Wyoming County Historians Office
The Torch- Attica High School yearbook,
*Wyoming County Veterans Services Office
*National WWII Memorial

Frank R. Whaley

2nd Lt., U. S. Army

Frank R. Whaley was born in Canada in 1916. His parents and siblings were born in New York. In 1920 they were living in Akron, NY. His father died of pneumonia on April 23, 1920 and his mother became ill shortly thereafter of the same illness. She recovered and moved back to Attica with her children where her family was. Frank's mother died almost the same day as his father twelve years later on April 22, 1932.

Orphaned now at 16, he went to live with his aunt and uncle in Attica where he attended high school. He graduated from Springfield College and became a clerk at the Young Woman's Bible School in Albany. He enlisted out of Albany on March 16, 1942 and became a graduate of Officers Candidate School in Fort Benning, GA in May of 1943. Three months later he married Alice Brown on August 14th while stationed at Camp Breckenridge, KY. He worked in the Division of Standard and Purchase.

Federalized with an Albany National Guard regiment, he was sent overseas in October of 1943 with the 141st Infantry Regiment, 36th Infantry. In April of 1944 his wife received notice that he had been reported missing since Feb. 11, 1944. By August he was declared dead by the War Department. He is buried in the Sicily-Rome American Cemetery, Nettuno, Italy in Plot H, Row 13, Grave 15. He was awarded a Purple Heart posthumously.

Survived by:
Wife: Alice Brown Whaley of 170 Eagle St., Albany, NY.
Parents: Harry and Maude Barnes Whaley (both deceased) of Akron, East Aurora and Attica.
Sister: Jean Whaley of 210 Northland Ave., Buffalo, NY.
Aunt & Uncle: Bessie Grile Barnes and Augustus "Duffy" Barnes.

*Attica News – April 29, 1920; February 26, 1942; August 21, 1944; April 6, 1944
*Buffalo Evening News – August 25, 1944
*Knickenbocker News, Albany, NY – August 14, 1943
*National WWII Memorial

Artell Francis Zahler Jr. aka Francis Artell Zahler Jr.

Pvt. 1st Class
U.S. Army

Artell Francis Zahler, or "Art" to his friends, was born in Attica on February 17, 1925. He graduated from St. Vincent's grade school and Attica High School. Art was in intramural sports all four years of high school including basketball, track and the Gym Exhibition. He was a member of the Science Club, Camera Club, orchestra and Music Night. A quote from his yearbook was, "The word rest is not in my vocabulary." He was attending Canisius College when he entered the service.

Artell joined the service April 6, 1943 with training at Fort Leonard Wood in the 290th Infantry, Co. B. In August he was transferred to engineering school at the University of Wyoming in Laramie, Wyoming. That September, he continued his studies at Iowa State College in Ames, Iowa. When the specialized program he was in was discontinued he was transferred back to the Infantry, Co. B. 380 Battalion at Fort Leonard Wood, MO. Later the battalion was moved to San Luis Obispo and then Camp Cook, both in California. They arrived in France on March 6, 1945. He served in the Dusseldorf and Ruhr Pocket areas and also in Germany.

While on a reconnoitering expedition for the 97th Division of Gen. Patton's Army in Czechoslovakia, he was killed in action April 30, 1945 while serving in the European Theater in Germany. His body was brought back in 1948 for burial in St. Vincent's Cemetery in Attica.

Survived by:
Parents: Artell and Ruth Noteman Zahler of Attica.
Sister: Alice Ann of Attica.

*Attica News – May 24, 1945; August, 1943; September 23, 1943
The Torch, Attica High School yearbook, 1942.

Image from *The Torch*, Attica High School yearbook, 1944

CHAPTER FOUR

Bennington

Charles R. Cannon
Sgt., U.S. Army

Charles R. Cannon was born in 1918. He graduated from Attica High School in 1937. In school he participated in track. A quote from his yearbook reads, "A gentleman is often seen, but seldom heard to laugh."

During his service he spent 18 months in Alaska constructing the Alcan (Alaska-Canada) highway. Charles went overseas in July of 1944 and saw action in France, Belgium and Germany including the Invasion of Brest and was awarded the Silver Star while serving with the 35th Engineer Combat Battalion, Co. C. He was one of the American soldiers who narrowly escaped death when the Ludendorff Bridge collapsed at Remagen, Germany.

Sergeant Cannon was killed in action during the crossing of the Rhine River, European Theater, Germany on March 25, 1945.

His family received the following decorations, the Silver Star, Purple Heart, Sharpshooters Award and the Good Conduct Medal.

The following is according to the *Batavia Daily News*, October 23, 1945: "Accompanying the Silver Star which was awarded for gallantry during the 'Battle of the Bulge,' was the following citation: While setting up road blocks and digging in his position, Sergeant Cannon heard approaching enemy tanks. Upon arriving at a point where he could see the advancing armor, his first bazooka team fired a shot which stopped the leading tank. The two tanks following immediately took up a

position and fired, scoring a direct hit on the second tank and rendering it useless throughout the remainder of the engagement.

"The tenacity of purpose, courage and zealous attention to duty demonstrated by Sergeant Cannon symbolize the highest traditions of the Armed Forces and reflect great credit upon himself.

"Sergeant Cannon's deeds mentioned in the citation saved the whole battalion, according to two buddies, Sergeant Claude Bliele of Gasport, and Sergeant Willard Hyde of Moira. They were with Sergeant Cannon during the almost four years of service. According to his buddies, the crossing was being affected in a rowboat in which were 12 men; three engineers and nine infantrymen. Only one escaped."

He is memorialized at Luxembourg American Cemetery and Memorial and has a headstone in Cowlesville Cemetery.

Survived by:
Parents: Raymond A. and Mae D. (Austin) Cannon of Bullis Rd. in Cowlesville, NY. (Mae was later a resident of Aurora Park Health Care in East Aurora, NY.)

**The Daily News, Batavia, NY.* – August 10, 1945; October 23, 1945
**Buffalo Evening News* – December 31, 1945
*Wyoming County Veterans Services Office
*The Torch, Attica High School Yearbook, 1937
*National WWII Memorial

*Note: a more detailed description of Sgt. Cannon's life, written by Malcolm Willard, was printed in the July 1995, Vol. 42 Issue #1 of *Historical Wyoming*.

Robert H. Summers

Pvt. 1st Class
U.S. Army

Robert H. Summers was born in 1920, a native of Buffalo, NY. He graduated from South Park High School and attended Canisius College for one year. He was employed as an Actor. In 1939 he joined the 121st Cavalry of the New York National Guard, which later was mechanized as the 102nd Coast Artillery Anti-Aircraft Regiment. He was later transferred to the 112th C.A. Transport Detachment.

He enlisted in the New York National Guard on January 6, 1941 prior to the war. In 1942 he transferred to the U.S. Air Force for pilot training at Pampa Air Field, Texas. His wife and five-month-old son lived in Bennington with her parents during Robert's service.

While at Pampa Air Field he qualified for Army Specialized Training and was sent to Vanderbilt University at Nashville, TN. The college was discontinued in April of 1943 and Robert was again reassigned; this time to the U.S. Army Infantry at Camp Atterbury, IN. He was sent overseas, serving with the 424th Infantry Regiment 106th Infantry Division.

On December 27, 1944, he was killed in action in Belgium during the battle with the Germans trying to crack the Allied Line.

Robert was buried at Henri-Chapelle American Cemetery and Memorial in Belgium in Plot C, Row 14 Grave 47. He was awarded the Bronze Star and a Purple Heart.

Survived by:
Wife: Helen Summers, Bennington
Son: 5-months-old, Robert (who became a sports writer for the *Buffalo Evening News.*)
Mother: Mrs. Estelle B. Summers and the late Judge Robert J. Summers of Buffalo, NY.
Brother: Pvt. William Summers, U.S. Marines
Sisters: Mrs. John W. Joyce Jr.; Mrs. John J. Troup Jr.; Mrs. Thomas V. Leary; Mrs. Louis Miller; and Eleanor Summers

Attica News – Thursday, January 25, 1945
Buffalo Courier Express – October 14, 1942
Buffalo Evening News – January 16, 1945
*National WWII Memorial

Image from *The Torch*, Attica High School yearbook, 1944

CHAPTER FIVE

Castile

Elmer J. Boatfield

Pvt. 1st Class
U.S. Army

Elmer J. Boatfield was born in 1909. He was a graduate of South Byron High School and Rochester Business Institute. He worked at Buffalo Arms Company. Elmer and his wife moved to Castile from Elba after purchasing a residence on Beechwood Ave.

He entered the service in January 8, 1944 and was sent overseas in July 1944.

Transferred to Infantry in December of 1944, Elmer underwent training in France then assigned to the 406th Infantry Regiment, Co. D 102nd Ozark Division of the 9th Army.

He saw action in Belgium and Holland. Elmer was awarded the Combat Infantryman's Badge and Good Conduct Ribbon just prior to his death.

He was killed in action on February 28, 1945 near Monchengladbach on the way to the Rhine in Germany.

He was buried in Grand View Cemetery in Batavia, NY.

Survived by:
Wife: Theodora M. Eddy Boatfield of Beechwood Ave. in Castile.
Mother: Mrs. Catherine (Cravan) Boatfield of Morganville, NY and the late John Boatfield who died in 1940.

Brother: Irving T. Boatfield of Batavia, NY.
Sisters: Mrs. Isabelle M. (Merton R.) Hoyt of Batavia, NY and Miss Barbara Boatfield of Morganville, NY.

The Castilian – Thursday, October 28, 1948
Perry Record – October 28, 1948
*National WWII Memorial website
*Wyoming County Veterans Services Office

Photo: Elmer Boatfield on left, brother Tommy on right.

Casimer Joseph Czerminski aka Kazimier Jozef Czerminski

Seaman 2nd Class
U.S. Navy

Casimer Joseph Czerwinski or by his birth certificate, Kazimier Jozef Czerminski was born December 18, 1893 at Sloan, NY. Casimer's father, John, was a carpenter who was born in Poland and his mother, born in Buffalo. They were living at Silver Lake, NY when he enlisted in the Navy in March of 1943.

He was listed as Missing in Action on July 10, 1943 as a result of action against the enemy on the *USS Maddox*. He was officially declared killed in action on July 11, 1944 near Sicily.

He is memorialized on the Tablets of the Missing in Sicily-Rome American Cemetery. He was posthumously awarded the Purple Heart.

Survived by:
Parents: Mr. and Mrs. John and Helen Czerminski of Castile.
Brothers: George, Henry, and Edwin at home; Chester J. Czerminski, Seaman 1st C, US Navy; Matthew H. Czerminski, PFC US Army.
Sisters: Alfreda, Susan and Louise, at home.

*Wyoming County Times-*February 7, 1946
Castilian- November 7, 1957
*Certificate of Birth
*Wyoming County Veterans Services Office
*National WWII Memorial

Kermit Adolph Davis

Cpl. T-5, U.S. Army

Kermit Adolph Davis was born on April 20, 1910 in Centerville, Allegany County, NY. He was employed at Worcester Salt Company in Silver Springs, NY for several years in the loading department before entering the service in April 8, 1943.

Kermit went overseas in November 23, 1944 and was a member of the 275th Engineers 75th Infantry Division in the Battle of St. Vith, Belgium.

There are conflicting dates of death in several newspapers giving December 31, 1944 or January 1, 1945 as the date.

He died when a land mine exploded by a jeep that he was driving. He died in a Belgium hospital the following day at the age of 34.

He was buried in a European cemetery, but after the war ended his body was among the first to be returned to the United States. The *Wyoming County Times* newspaper dated November 27, 1947 reads "Burial services for the remains of T-5 Kermit Davis were held in Hope Cemetery on Sunday afternoon at 2:30 o'clock before a large assemblage of people who solemnly paid final tribute to one of Castile's war heroes.

The services were conducted by Wallace-Jeffers American Legion, with full military rites being accorded the dead soldier who gave his life on a European battlefield in the defense of his country."

Survived by:
Wife: Norma E. Davis of Castile.
Daughter: Katherine Irene Davis – born after he was killed
Mother: Mrs. Rena Davis of Greece, NY.
Brothers: Harold C. Davis of Arcade, NY and Cpl. Gerald Davis of Fort McClellan, Alabama.
Sister: Mrs. Alice Schuknecht of Greece, NY.

*Wyoming County Times – February 8, 1945; November 27, 1947
*Perry Herald – January 3, 1946, November 27, 1947
*The Greece Press, Rochester, NY. – February 1, 1945
*Rochester Times Union – January 27, 1945
*Wyoming County Veterans Services Office

Willard T. DeGolyer

2nd Lt., U.S. Army Air Corps

Willard T. DeGolyer was born March 7 1914. He graduated from Perry High School in 1934. He received the Alumni cup symbolic of the most all-around student. He was President of his class in his junior year. He starred in football, basketball and baseball.

He entered into Cornell University in the fall of 1936 where he served as treasurer of the Student Council in his senior year and was elected to the university's honor society. After graduation in 1940, he worked several months for the Production Credit Association in Batavia.

Willard joined the Army Air Corps in October 1940. He trained in Lakeland Florida, and at Maxwell Field Montgomery, Alabama where he earned his wings and was commissioned 2nd Lt. He was married on June 5, 1941 to Edith Cecil Carson. Around June 20th, 1941 he was assigned for duty in Puerto Rico for two years.

In February 9, 1942 while serving as an instructor at Gunter Field Montgomery, Alabama for American and English Cadets, Willard and RAF Cadet Reginald Price of London, England were both killed while making an emergency landing some miles from the air base, he was 27. He was buried in Grace Cemetery in Castile.

After Willard's death, Richard Comfort wrote an editorial in the *Perry Herald* about Willard, closing it with a quote from a poem by Hervey Allen;

"Christ Jesus when I come to die.
Grant me a clean, sweet summer sky..."

Survived by:
Wife: Edith Cecil (Carson) DeGolyer
Parents: Mr. and Mrs. C. Scott and Florence DeGolyer of Castile.
Brothers: Avery and Calvin DeGolyer
Sister: Mrs. Betty Neiderhauser of Ithaca, NY.

*Perry Herald – June 4, 1941; February 11, 1942
*The Castilian – February 12, 1942
**Historical Wyoming*, July 1995, Vol. 42 No. 1, page 27
*Wyoming County Veterans Services Office

George M. Hickey

Pvt., U. S. Army

George M. Hickey was born at Silver Lake, NY on August 30, 1909. They were living in the Perry village part of Castile according to the 1910 census. By 1920 George was a resident of Allegany County living with his mother and brother, his parents having divorced. He was employed as a driller in the Allegany and Bradford oil fields in Bolivar. George married Rena Miori on October 11, 1937 and had two children. They divorced prior to his enlistment.

He was inducted into the Army in December of 1942 stationed in Camp Chaffee, Arkansas before being transferred to Camp Campbell in

Kentucky. On June 27, 1944, while on maneuvers at Camp Campbell in the fortified area at Casey Creek, he was accidentally killed when someone walked into a trip wire setting off a parachute flare which burst in Pvt. Hickey's face. He was immediately taken to the Station Hospital at Camp Campbell but his wounds were so extensive he was dead on arrival. He was accompanied home by train to Wellsville by Sgt. Arthur Spring and brought to the Loop Funeral Home in Bolivar, Allegany County, NY. Burial was in Maple Lawn Cemetery in Bolivar.

Survived by:
Former Wife: (divorced) Rena (Miori) Hickey of Olean, NY.
Children: Frances and Dolores, at home.
Father: Frank Hickey of Perry, NY.
Mother: the late Mrs. Julia (Elmer) Hickey of Bolivar, NY. (Parents were divorced. Julia married 2nd Arthur H. Mastin and 3rd Fred Maynard. She died March of 1944.)
Brother: Harold Hickey of Friendship, NY.

**Olean Times Union* – June 30, 1944
**Perry Record* – July 6, 1944
**Bolivar Breeze* – July 6, 1944
**New York State Marriage Index, 1937,* #52011
**1910 Federal Census,* Town of Castile, Village of Perry.

John Walter Holmes

Pvt., U. S. Army

John W. Holmes was born in Utica, NY on February 26, 1924, the son of Walter and Lillian Holmes. He attended Gloversville High School where he had been an athlete on the football, baseball, and basketball teams. He had come to Castile, NY in 1941 and lived there until his induction into the Army in April 1943.

John went into service in April being a member of Company C, 193rd Glider Infantry, 17th Airborne Division. On November 17, 1943 at Camp Mackall, North Carolina he was killed at age 19 by the accidental explosion of an artillery 37mm shell. One of the soldiers had found a live shell on the artillery range and smuggled it into the barracks. While examining the shell, it dropped onto the floor and exploded filling the barracks with flying shrapnel.

Pvt. Holmes was lying on his bunk, several feet away, reading his mail and was perusing the last letter, written by his mother when the explosion occurred. A piece of shrapnel struck him at the base of the spine, severing the large artery in that region. Camp medical authorities stated that death caused by a severe hemorrhage took place in approximately three minutes.

The official information did not disclose whether any of the other 47 soldiers quartered in the barracks were harmed. He was buried in Graceland Cemetery in Albany, NY.

Survived by:
Fiancé: Miss Evelyn L. Poole of Castile.
Mother: Mrs. Lillian Pound of Albany, NY.
Maternal Grandmother: Mrs. Louise Walker of Gloversville, NY.
Aunt: Mrs. C. Scott DeGolyer of Castile.

*Wyoming County Times - July 25, 1945
*Perry Herald – November 24, 1943
*Perry Record – December 2, 1943
*The Castilian - December 2, 1943

Merrill T. Spring

1st Lt., U. S. Army Air Forces

Merrill T. Spring was born October 16, 1918 in New Jersey. He had lived in East Aurora, NY for a time but his father lived in Castile.

He enlisted in January of 1941. After a year in the Armored Division at Camp Polk, Louisiana, he was accepted as an air cadet and began his training.

He was on an Army Air Force Bombardier of a B-29 when the plane was shot down over a German occupied sector in France on July 6, 1944. He was captured while making an effort to rescue other members of his American crew who were trapped in the flaming aircraft after it was forced down behind enemy lines. He died in a German Prison Camp on August 3, 1944 of severe burns from the attempted rescue. His place of burial was in Germany. His father stated in a newspaper article, "He did not intend to request return of Merrill's body," and, "let him rest in peace." His father accepted a posthumous Purple Heart award and citation made by President Truman for his son. Mr. Spring said he would not return the medal awarded his son even though he did not agree with the President's policies. He stated, "This would not be in keeping with the spirit of the boy... It was America and not for any one man for whom my son died."

However, in a untitled newspaper article dated 1952 it reads: "The body of First Lieut. Merrill T. Spring of Castile, Air Force hero killed during World War II, will be returned for burial in an East Aurora cemetery near his mother and brother." The name of the cemetery is Oakwood Cemetery, East Aurora, NY.

Survived by:
Father: Frank E. Spring
Mother: Mrs. Amanda K. Spring of East Aurora, NY.

Buffalo Evening News – July 30, 1942
Perry Record – January 24, 1952
Buffalo Courier Express – November 8, 1944
The Daily News, Batavia – September 20, 1944

Washington, D.C. Detail of a B-29 bombing plane on public view at the National Airport. *Library of Congress*

CHAPTER SIX

Covington

Robert J. Boatfield

Pvt., U.S. Army Air Forces

Robert J. Boatfield was born on April 30, 1920 in the hamlet of Pearl Creek, town of Covington, to William and Amy Boatfield. When Robert's father died in 1925, he made his home with Mrs. Taylor (a sister) and his paternal aunt and uncle, Mr. and Mrs. Floyd Paine, on a farm on Perry-Pavilion road. He lived in Covington for nearly 15 years prior to his enlistment.

He was a member of the Young People's Class of the Covington church and the Youth Fellowship. He attended Covington District School No. 6 and Pavilion Central School.

He enlisted in the Army Air Corps at Buffalo, NY on January 15, 1940. From there he went to Fort Slocum, where he stayed for ten weeks and was then sent to Fort McDowell in California and from there to the Presidio in California.

He reached the Philippines on June 24, 1940. Here he served with the 19th Air Base Squadron, at Nichols Field, Rizal P.I, a suburb of Manila. According to radio reports, Private Boatfield and other airmen in his squadron were merged with the 31st Infantry on Bataan, Island of Luzon, because the depleted air force could no longer function on its own. The 31st Infantry were all taken prisoner on April 9, 1942 on Bataan by the Japanese, along with thousands of other U.S. servicemen.

Over a year later his sister Clair received word by telegram from the war department that Robert died after 13 months in a Prisoner of War Camp in the Philippines on May 12, 1943. His remains were not recovered but he is memorialized at Manila American Cemetery, Fort Bonifacio, Manila, Philippines. He was a recipient of the Prisoner of War Medal and the Purple Heart, posthumously.

Survived by:
Father: William Boatfield who died in 1925.
Mother: Amy (Gates) Boatfield (who later married Joseph Ravadeau). She died November 14, 1941 in Munning, MI.
Brother: Charles Boatfield of Seneca Falls, NY and William Boatfield of Syracuse, NY.
Sisters: Mrs. Catherine Taylor of Bergen, NY; Mrs. Gladys Tracy and Evelyn Boatfield both of Rochester, NY; and Mrs. Mildred Houseman of Battle Creek, MI.
Foster Brothers: John C. and Paul W. Paine both of Covington.
Foster Sister: Miriam Gail Paine of Covington.

*Perry Herald – May 20, 1942; June 2, 1945
*National WWII Memorial website

*Note: For more insight into what Private Boatfield and the men of Bataan endured as Japanese prisoners of war, see a story written by the author entitled Freedom Is Not Free. It is a biography of Sgt. William Knight (whose excerpt is in this book); a story of a soldier's three year trial as a Japanese P.O.W. in the Philippines and the Japanese homeland. The account is on file at the Wyoming County Historian's Office, 26 Linwood Avenue in Warsaw and the Warsaw Public Library.

Jack McGee

Pvt. 1ˢᵗ Class, U.S. Army

Jack McGee was born July 9, 1921 in Perry, NY. He lived in Perry until 1931 when the family moved to Pearl Creek in the town of Covington where he graduated from Pavilion Central School in 1940. While in school, he had been involved with the senior play called *Easy Money*, the F. F. A., Student Council, track, and Dramatic Club. A quote by his senior picture reads, "I am slow of study but quick of play." He worked at Curtiss Wright Aircraft Factory in Buffalo before entering the service.

He was stationed in Camp Blanding, FL, and afterwards, Fort Meade, in Maryland. In September, 1944 he joined Company M, 3rd Battalion, 157th Infantry Regiment, 45th Infantry Division, 7th Army. His military occupational specialty was heavy machine gunner (605). He was awarded the Combat Infantryman badge in October of 1944 for "exemplary conduct in action against the enemy."

In July of 1944, he was sent overseas and saw action in several campaigns in Italy and France. In April 1945 they were in Germany where they liberated the infamous Dachau Concentration Camp outside of Munich. On May 8, 1945 Germany surrendered.

On May 19, 1945, eleven days after the Germans surrendered, he was injured while on duty. He was sent to the 93rd Evacuation Hospital in Munich, but his injuries were too severe to save his life. A letter informed the parents that he was killed in a non-combat accident near Munich at the age of 23.

He was buried in a temporary military cemetery in Reutti, Germany. In 1948 his body was then moved to Lorraine American Cemetery and Memorial in Saint Avold, France. A bronze plaque in St. Mary's Cemetery in Pavilion is in memory of Jack. He was awarded the Bronze Star, posthumously.

Survived by:
Parents: Elmer J. and Marjorie McGee of Pearl Creek.
Brothers: Francis McGee of Buffalo, NY; Robert McGee of Fillmore, NY; Tech. Sgt. Richard McGee; England; and Vincent McGee, Merchant Marine, Stationed at Sheepshead Bay, LI.
Sisters: Mildred E. Powers of Pearl Creek; Mary, who died in 1936 at age 16 in an automobile accident.

*Perry Record – June 13, 1944; June 7, 1945
**Rochester Times Union* – June 7, 1945
**Western New Yorker* -June 14, 1945
*Wyoming County Veterans Services Office
*A biography paper compiled by Richard Hey, February, 2018, with commentary and family history provided by John Powers.

CHAPTER SEVEN

Eagle

Jesse C. Ballard

Pvt. 1st Class
U.S. Army

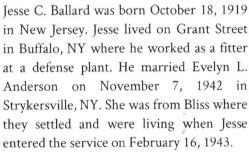

Jesse C. Ballard was born October 18, 1919 in New Jersey. Jesse lived on Grant Street in Buffalo, NY where he worked as a fitter at a defense plant. He married Evelyn L. Anderson on November 7, 1942 in Strykersville, NY. She was from Bliss where they settled and were living when Jesse entered the service on February 16, 1943.

Pvt. Ballard was killed in action on August 2, 1944, while fighting the Japanese in Myitkyina, Burma. There is a Memorial headstone which is in National Memorial Cemetery of the Pacific in Honolulu, Hawaii in Plot B, 204.

Survived by:
Wife: Evelyn L. (Anderson) Ballard Buck of Bliss.
Parents: John Ballard and Nora (Crane) Ballard
Brother: Herman L. Ballard

*Transcript from Register of Marriages in the Town of Eagle
*Wyoming County Veterans Services Office
*National WWII Memorial website

Robert J. Hess

Sgt., U.S. Army

Robert J. Hess was born in Bliss, NY on March 5, 1921. He became the art editor of the school paper as well as an accomplished athlete.

Robert played in the school and town bands and was a member of the school dance orchestra, which he helped organize. In 1939 he was the salutatorian of his graduating class from Bliss High School. He went on to Geneseo State Teachers College where he studied for two years with the desire to become a teacher.

Bob Hess on right, Bill Munger on left.

He entered the service on July 3, 1942 from Buffalo. He attained the rank of sergeant and qualified for Officers' Training School. For several months he attended Lafayette College in Easton, PA. Robert was returned to the infantry as a private when the government closed all such training programs. He was sent to Europe on September 19, 1944. Just prior to his death, he again received a sergeant's rating. He served with the 335 Infantry 84 Division.

He was killed on December 16, 1944 in Germany, becoming the fourth boy from Bliss to be killed in action. Robert is buried in the Wethersfield Cemetery.

Survived by:
Parents: Thomas and Blanche (Morgan) Hess of Bliss.
Brothers: James, Richard and Kermit of Bliss.
Sisters: Charlotte Hess of Bliss; Mrs. Floyd Tobey of Niagara Falls, NY.

Perry Herald – January 3, 1945; February 2, 1945
Wyoming County Times – April 25, 1945.
*Wyoming County Veterans Services Office

Warren George Kader

Staff Sgt., U.S. Army

Warren George Kader was born on May 25, 1921 in the town of Eagle and graduated from Bliss High School, class of 1938.

He entered the service in July 17, 1942 and was sent to Camp Gruber, OK, then onto maneuvers in Louisiana and finally to Fort Houston, TX. Warren went overseas in the fall of 1943 to North Africa for about six weeks. He went on to Italy in February of 1944, and was killed in action there on May 12, 1944. He was in the 350th Infantry, 88th Division, 5th Army under General Clark.

Capt. Thomas L. Cussans, a friend in the service tells of his death.

"Dear Sir,

I received your letter regarding Warren and will attempt to answer it the best I can. Warren was one of the finest soldiers I have ever known and his loss has been deeply felt by myself and the company. I'm sorry I can't go on writing all the nice things I know about Warren because of the little time I have to write. I do hope you can understand my feelings as I have lived with him nearly two years and in that time he has been like my own brother. I just know you will understand, as it is hard to put any feelings in words.

My company was occupying a hill we had taken and everything was under control. Warren was moving his squad to the top of the hill when they came under shell fire. The men quickly dispersed and Warren and two other men got in an old house that was near. They were observed going into the house and received a hit. Warren was killed instantly. The aid men were there immediately and I believe that concussion had more to do with it than anything else.

Warren's package did arrive and it was returned in the A.P.O. I imagine unless the package had food in it, that it will be returned to you. All of his personal articles were taken by the proper people.

I hope this letter will help some and if I haven't answered enough questions don't be afraid to write. I will do everything possible that is asked by you so if there is any doubt in your mind, write.

Yours,

Capt. Thomas L. Cussans"

The body of Warren was escorted home by Pfc. Arthur L. Steinstra for burial in the Lyonsburg Cemetery in Bliss on September 2, 1948.

Survived by:
Fiancé: Miss Madge Roberts, also of Bliss.
Parents: Joseph and Hazel Kader of Bliss.
Sisters: Edith and Edna Kader at home; Mrs. Lillian Buttles of Fillmore (or Pike); and Mrs. Thelma Stalhacker of Rochester, NY.
Brother: Laverne Kader at home.

*ced*Perry Herald* – June 16, 1944
**Wyoming County Times* – June 15, 1944; July 13, 1944
*Unknown clipping – September 30, 1948
*Wyoming County Veterans Services Office

LaVerne Paul Rissinger

Lt., U.S. Army Air Forces

LaVerne Paul Rissinger was born February 9, 1917, in Gainesvilles, NY. He graduated from Bliss High School in 1933. He was a member of the Hermitage Baptist church and the Pike Masonic Lodge. He was employed by the Buffalo Forge Company before his enlistment.

He entered the service in June of 1941 and received training as an engineer along with officers training in the Army Air Force. He served one year in the U.S. Engineers Corps at Ft. Belvoir, VA. In April of 1942, Lt. Rissinger enlisted in the U.S.A.A.F. where, he received his wings. Aviation Cadet

Rissinger was commissioned as a Second Lieutenant on March 25, 1943 at Moody Field, GA, where he completed his training as the pilot of a Flying Fortress. In early October he was sent overseas.

He was killed when his plane crashed in Bovingdon, Hart, England on December 9, 1943. He was the first war casualty from Bliss.

His burial was in Maple Grove Cemetery in Gainesville.

Survived by:
Parents: Paul and Marjorie (Reed) Rissinger of 103 Virginia Rd. in Williamsville, NY.
Sister: Mrs. Clarice Sanford, Williamsville, NY. (LKA Clarice Hawks of Arcade)

Western New Yorker – January 6, 1944
Perry Herald – February 24, 1949
*Wyoming County Veterans Services Office
*Stanley Rutherford, former Gainesville Historian's Notebook

Floyd Kermit Roberts

Pvt., U.S. Army

Floyd K. Roberts was born in the town of Eagle on August 19, 1916 to Thomas and Lucia (Watson) Roberts. He attended Bliss High School and for several years worked in Fillmore, NY. He had announced his engagement to Miss Florine Minard before he entered the army. He was fond of reading and with the rare ability of being able to write extremely well of all that interested him.

Floyd better known as "Curly" by his friends, entered the service in February 7, 1941 at Fillmore and received his training at Fort Knox and Fort Benning. In June 1943, he went overseas. He was in the Italian Invasion, serving in France at Normandy, and in Belgium was in the First Army under General Patton. He had been in duty in North Africa and England. He was an artillery observer with Battery A, 58th Armored Field Artillery, 1st Army, under General Hodges. His last letter home told of his receiving word that his mother had died in November.

His parents were originally notified the beginning of February 1945, that Floyd was declared as Missing in Action. Later the same week, however they received word that he had been killed. It would be confirmed that he was taken prisoner of war by the German Army.

On December 22, 1944 while preparing for a general retreat from Belgium, a horrible atrocity was committed by the German Army. Approximately 150 American soldiers—all prisoners and all subject to and deserving the rights and fair treatment of P.O.W.s rendered by the General Rules of War— were all herded together and murdered by machine gun fire by German soldiers. This atrocity was well documented after the war by an investigation into war crimes.

Floyd is buried Luxembourg American Cemetery, Luxembourg Plot 1, Row 11, Grave 20. There is also a headstone in the Pine Grove Cemetery in Fillmore, Allegany County, NY that was dedicated as a memorial to him.

Survived by:
Fiancé: Florine Minard
Parents: Thomas and Lucia Roberts, both deceased. (Mrs. Roberts name appears as Lucia on Floyd's birth certificate but as Flora in some newspaper articles.)
Sisters: Mrs. Agnes Dornan of Bliss and Mrs. Nina Campbell of Portageville, NY.
Brothers: Elliot Roberts and Lewis Roberts, both of Bliss; Palmer Roberts of Gainesville, NY; Grant Roberts of Perry, NY;
Half Brothers: Frank Roberts of Perry and Irving Roberts of Hume, NY.

*Perry Herald – February 9, 1945
**Wyoming County Times* – February 8, 1945
*Perry Record – February 8, 1945; February 7, 1945
**Rochester Times Union* – February 8, 1945
*Wyoming County Veterans Services Office
*Verified Transcript from the Register of Births

CHAPTER EIGHT

Gainesville

Edward James Courtney

Pvt. U.S. Marine Corps

Edward James Courtney was born May 19, 1921 in the village of Silver Springs, town of Gainesville, the son of Ellen Courtney and the late Edward Courtney. During his high school days he was involved in athletics and pitched for the high school baseball league. After graduating from Silver Springs School in 1939, he had taken training at the NYA School in Auburn. He worked briefly at the Buffalo Arms Company in Cheektowaga, NY.

He enlisted in the Marine Corps in Buffalo on January 30, 1942 and was stationed at Parris Island and Quantico, VA.

After being in the service about two months Ed came home on a three day leave to spend Easter with his family. He was involved in an automobile accident on Groveland road with three other marines who were on leave with him from Quantico. The car in which he was a passenger went around a curve, lost control and struck a tree. It was believed the wet road and unfamiliarity of the area by the driver, led to the accident.

Sgt. Courtney's family was able to be with him when he died in Dansville hospital about four hours later on April 4, 1942. The other three occupants with him were also killed. He was the first Silver Springs boy in service to lose his life. The funeral was held from St.

Mary's Church in Silver Springs on April 7th with burial in St. Mary's Cemetery.

Survived by:
Parents: Ellen E. (Sullivan) Courtney of 26 Church St. in Silver Springs, and the late Edward James Courtney
Brother: John James Courtney, at home.
Sister: Eleanor Courtney.
Two half-brothers: Gordon Cody of Silver Springs; and Pvt. Leo F. Cody, U.S. Army.
Half-sister: Mary Ellen Chastek Jr. of Silver Springs.
(The other three officers killed were: driver and owner of the car, Sgt. John W. Lenahan, 18, of Buffalo; Pvt. William Kenny, 20, also of Buffalo; and Pvt. Harold J. Keyes, 31, of Niagara Falls.)

Perry Herald – April 8, 1942
Wyoming County Times – April 9, 1942
*Mary E. Mann, Gainesville Historian

Robert Chasey Dumbleton

1st Lt., U.S. Army Air Forces

BOMBER PILOT

Lieut. Robert C. Dumbleton

Robert Chasey Dumbleton was born March 15, 1921 in Silver Springs and graduated from Silver Springs High School in 1939. He was prominent in athletics in both baseball and basketball. He had earned the highest rank in scouting, that of Eagle Scout to which he added the gold and bronze palm. He participated in the national jamboree held in Washington in 1937. In 1938 he joined the Methodist church and became an active Christian worker, serving a number of offices in the local church and Sunday school. He helped organize a Boy Scout troop in the Methodist church, becoming scoutmaster of Troop 53 at the time of his enlistment.

He was employed at Litteer's market and Keeney's grocery store in Warsaw until he entered the service.

He enlisted as an Air Cadet at Buffalo on January 23, 1942. He trained at Maxwell Field, AL; Arcadia, FL; Bush Field, GA and receiving his silver wings as a pilot and his 2nd Lt. Commission at Napier Field, AL on January 14, 1943. He then received advanced training in New Mexico and Kansas before leaving for combat duty May 15, 1943 with the 13th Air Force.

Over the next few months he served as a co-pilot on a bomber in the South Pacific, he flew over 40 combat missions, was promoted to 1st Lt. in October 1943 and earned the Air Medal with Six Oak Leaf clusters for his skill and bravery. He served with the 372nd Bomber Squadron, 307th Bomber Group.

Lt. Dumbleton had just passed his 23rd birthday and had written to his parents that he had been having a wonderful time on a fishing trip while he was on a rest period. On March 20, 1944 as a passenger aboard a transport plane returning from leave in Auckland, New Zealand, his plane crashed somewhere in the Pacific and all aboard were killed. An extensive search was made by sea and aircraft but could not be found.

In one of his last letters to his mother, Robert said these words:
"It is time for Taps," he wrote, "and I am ready."
Yet when he penned these words he little knew,
How soon, Death's Angel signaling his spirit
Would sound eternal Taps, the while he flew.

He is memorized at the Manila American Cemetery in Fort Bonifacio, Manila, Philippines. A memorial service also took place in Silver Springs and a bronze plaque is in place there in Elmwood Cemetery.

Survived by:
Parents: Lloyd F. and Elizabeth Dumbleton of Silver Springs
Brothers: Basil, Jack and Richard, at home; Donald, in the service.

The Castilian – May 25, 1944
Perry Herald – January 12, 1944; April 19, 1944
Perry Record – May 3, 1944; May 4, 1944
Wyoming County Times – May 25, 1944
Western New Yorker – February 1, 1945
*Record of the Town of Gainesville
*Notebook of Stanley Rutherford, former Gainesville Historian
*Wyoming County Veterans Services Office

James Gell

Pvt. 1st Class, U.S. Army

James Gell was born June 18, 1921 in Gainesville. He attended Silver Springs High School before he entered the service in Buffalo on July 3, 1942.

He trained at Camp Gruber, OK and in Louisiana. He was sent overseas in December of 1943. He served with the 351st Infantry, 88th Division in North Africa, Sicily and Italy.

During his service in the Mediterranean, he had been wounded in the leg during a battle in Italy and was awarded the Purple Heart. He recovered and returned to active duty in Italy where he was killed in action on July 26, 1944.

His body was returned home where a memorial service was held at the Methodist Church. The advance of colors was conducted by the American Legion with a Gold Star Citation delivered to the parents by Commander Roe B. Seaman. He was buried in Elmwood Cemetery, Silver Springs on June 7, 1949.

Survived by:
Parents: Thomas and Rhoda Gell of Silver Springs.
Brothers: Custer Gell of Castile, NY; Dean Gell of Silver Springs; Cpl. Arthur Gell and Pfc. Melvin Gell both of the U.S. Army stationed in France.
Sisters: Betty Gell and Shirley Gell, at home; Mrs. Marion Milgate of Arcade, NY; Mrs. Ethel Green of Silver Springs; Mrs. Dorothy Andrews of Perry, NY; Mrs. Lillian Rood of Attica, NY; and Mrs. Violet Strathearn of Wyoming, NY.

Perry Herald – May 13, 1944; August 16, 1944; December 4, 1944
The Castilian – June 16, 1949
Perry Record – June 16, 1949
*Wyoming County Veterans Services Office

Paul Clayton Husted

2nd Lt., U.S. Army Air Forces

Paul Clayton Husted was born in Silver Springs on April 10, 1923. As a 1941 graduate of Silver Springs High School he was valedictorian of his class. A very promising young man, he was awarded a scholarship to attend Eastman School of Music in Rochester, NY which he attended for two years. He was an accomplished violinist playing in many public places, both in Rochester, NY and in Houston, Texas. He was an active Boy Scout, attending the National Boy Scout Jamboree at Washington in 1937. In 1940 he was chosen by the American Legion to be a delegate to the Empire Boys State in Syracuse, NY.

As an active member of Silver Springs Methodist church he was involved in youth work and the choir.

Paul enlisted in the Air Corp as a cadet on November 7, 1942 in Rochester and called to active duty in March 1943. On Christmas Day 1943 he was engaged to Miss Gertrude Ruth White of Rochester.

Paul trained at Keesler Field, MS, Ellington Field, TX and University of Toledo, Santa Anna, CA and Drew Field, FL. He received his navigator's wings and a commission as second lieutenant in exercises from Ellington Field on May 20, 1944.

He was assigned to a Flying Fortress Squadron with the 15th Air Forces, as a navigator in their B-17 from U.S. to Newfoundland to Africa to Italy arriving about the middle of August 1944.

As a result of wounds received in his 13th mission in action over Vienna, Austria he died and was buried on August 28, 1944 in Italy. His body was returned home in November of 1948 for burial in Elmwood Cemetery. The local businesses closed during the funeral in his honor.

The Presidential Citation, signed by President Roosevelt, says, "He stands in the unbroken line of patriots who have dared to die that freedom might live, and grow and increase its blessings. Freedom lives, and through it, he lives – in a way that humbles the undertakings of most men."

Survived by:
Parents: Clayton L. & Elizabeth R. Husted of Silver Springs.

*Perry Herald – September 13, 1944; December 2, 1948
*Perry Record – September 14 & 28, 1944; November 28, 1944; January 11, 1945
*Wyoming County Veterans Services Office

Basil Numack

Staff Sgt., U.S. Army Air Forces

Basil Numack was born on March 9, 1925 in Hamtramck, Michigan. At the age of three his parents moved to the village of Silver Springs, in Gainesville where he attended school. He later attended NYA School in Auburn, NY where he took up sheet metal work and blue print reading. After completing the course he gained employment at the Warsaw Elevator Works. At night he studied for his correspondence course in drafting. He was nearly completed when he got the call to serve.

He was inducted on January 11, 1944 at Buffalo, NY. Before leaving the states, he circled Silver Springs with his "beautiful bomber" so his parents could see him fly.

In May of 1944 he came home for a 15 day furlough. He had just graduated from a Gunnery class at the Army Air Field in Las Vegas, NV. At the end of his furlough he reported at a replacement center at Lincoln, NE.

Upon completing training at Rapid City, SD each member of Numack's crew received an identification bracelet for having one of the best training records. Basil went overseas in September of 1944 with the 418th Bombardment Squadron in the 100th Bombardment Group known as the Bloody Hundred. He immediately put his training into action chalking up several flights in his few short months.

In his last letter to his parents on the 30th of December, he said he was writing a big letter to all his friends at the Elevator to thank them for their Christmas gifts that they had sent him. He said he felt very tired and would finish tomorrow. He never got the chance to finish the letter for the following day his plane was shot down.

His parents received word early in 1945 that he was reported Missing in Action on December 31, 1944 as a result of his aircraft being struck in midair over Zeven, Germany. His parents heard no further word except from the families of fellow crew members.

In May of 1946 Basil's parents were informed that he had indeed died on that day when his Flying Fortress was shot out of the sky. Confiscated German records showed that his remains had been recovered and buried on January 1, 1945 in Wesseloh Cemetery, Germany. After the war ended his remains were re-entered in Plot A, Row 27, Grave 6, in Ardennes-American Cemetery, Belgium.

On December 5, 1945 he had received the Air Medal with one Oak Leaf Cluster and the Citation of Honor "for meritorious achievement while participating in heavy bombardment missions in the air offensive against the enemy over Continental Europe. The courage, coolness, and skill displayed by this enlisted man upon these occasions reflected great credit upon himself and the armed forces of the United States." He was awarded the Purple Heart posthumously.

Survived by:
Parents: Walter and Marie (Hudick) Numack of Silver Springs.

Western New Yorker – March 21, 1946; May 9, 1946
Perry Herald – January 31, 1945; May 15, 1946; May 24, 1944
*Wyoming County Veterans Services Office
*100th BG Foundation, *www.100thbg.com*

Thomas Patrick O'Brien

Pvt., U.S. Army

Thomas Patrick O'Brien was born in White Haven, Pennsylvania on January 4, 1926. At the age of 1½, he moved to Silver Springs with his mother and older brother, Edward. They lived for several years with his grandparents Mr. and Mrs. John G. Robson. Thomas attended Silver Springs High School. Later, around 1939, the family moved into an apartment in the Weed Block. He worked at the Worcester Salt Plant until he turned 18 and enlisted in the army. While waiting to be called up for active service he worked odd jobs around the village and worked for several farmers in the area.

He entered the service on April 26, 1944. He was first stationed at Camp Dix in New Jersey then went to Camp Croft in South Carolina for his infantry training. In September he spent a ten day furlough at home after which time he reported to Camp Shelby, MS where he was scheduled to receive warfare training until March, 1945. However, in early November of 1944, he was sent to an embarkation camp. He served with the 330th Infantry Regiment, 83rd Infantry Division. The last of November, word was received by his mother of his arrival in England but was there only a short time. On January 3, 1945, "Tommy" wrote his mother that he was somewhere in Belgium.

He lost his life at the Battle of the Bulge in Belgium on January 17, 1945, at the age 19. He is buried in Henri-Chapelle American Cemetery Plot C, Row 11, Grave 11. A memorial service was held on September 30, 1945 at the Silver Springs Methodist Church. He received the Purple Heart and a Presidential Citation posthumously.

Survived by:
Mother: Mrs. Bertha P. (Robson) O'Brien of Silver Springs (and father Thomas H. O'Brien, deceased)
Brother: Edward O'Brien, G.M. 2 Cl. U.S. Navy on the *USS Wyoming*.
Grandparents: Mr. and Mrs. John G. Robson of Whiton Ave. in Silver Springs.

*Perry Herald – October 4, 1945
**Western New Yorker* – February 22, 1945
*Newspaper articles, paper and dates unknown
*Wyoming County Veterans Services Office

Henry P. Schell

Pvt., U.S. Army

Henry P. Schell was born in July 29, 1913 in Germany. He was employed at Curtiss-Wright. He married Lorraine Gloss (born May 30, 1914) on March 28, 1936 in Buffalo, daughter of Samuel and Catherine (Cragan) Gloss. He moved with his family from Buffalo, NY to Gainesville a few months before entering the service at Buffalo on February 23, 1944.

He was sent overseas shortly after basic training and served in the European Theater. On February 19, 1945 he was killed in action at the age of 31 in Luxembourg, Germany while serving as a spotter with his infantry unit the 5th Signal Company, 5th Infantry Division. He was 31 years of age. He is buried in the Luxembourg American Cemetery, Luxembourg in Plot E, Row 11, Grave 12.

Survived by:
Wife: Mrs. Lorraine (Gloss) Schell; North Gainesville.
Children: Betty Jane, Richard, Henry, Carol, Beverly, and Robert.

Parents: Emil and Helen (Flick) Schell; Buffalo, NY moved to Gainesville by 1947.
Brother: Emil C. Schell Jr., Seaman Second Class, USNR in Newport, Rhode Island
Sister: Mrs. Mary Buckwalt

Western New Yorker – April 5, 1945
Wyoming County Times – March 8, 1945
Wyoming Reporter – October 26, 1950
Warsaw Pennysaver – November 11, 2012
*Wyoming County Veterans Services Office

Walter W. Shearing
Tech. Sgt., U.S. Army

Walter W. Shearing was born in Gainesville on March 9, 1918. He attended Gainesville High School. The youngest of five, he never married. He sprayed potatoes in the fields for local farmers and was employed by the Buffalo Arms Corporation before entering the service. He was a member of Gainesville Fire Department.

On March 5, 1942, he was inducted as a Private and steadily rose to his rank of T. Sergeant. He had service with the 324th Infantry Regiment, 44th Infantry Division. Since September of 1944, he had been awarded the Bronze Star twice with one Oak Leaf Cluster and the Combat Infantry badge having served in combat in Europe. He was killed by a sniper while serving with the 7th Army on April 17, 1945 in Germany at the age of 26.

An extract from the Commanding Officer's letter to his mother read, "Walter died without suffering and has been buried in the United States Military Cemetery at Bensheim, Germany. Appropriate religious services were held at his grave by a Protestant Chaplain of the United

States Army. Walter gave his life for the liberty and freedom of all of us. He was a good soldier, he was well liked, and his name will always be cherished by those who fought with him and beside him."

He was reburied at the Lorraine American Cemetery & Memorial in France in Plot D, Row 20, Grave 37. His name has also been included on his parent's tombstone in Maple Grove Cemetery in Gainesville in his memory. The Purple Heart was awarded to his mother posthumously.

Survived by:
Parents: Mrs. Zaida Shearing and the late Herbert S. Shearing
Sister: Mrs. Dorothy VanSlyke of Mills Mills.
Brothers: Donald Shearing and Arthur Shearing of Gainesville; Robert Shearing of Rock Glen in Gainesville.

Wyoming County Times – May 10, 1945
*Wyoming County Veterans Services Office
*National WWII Memorial

John H. Smith

Captain, U.S. Army

John H. Smith was born July 21, 1918. He was a graduate of Gainesville High School and Houghton College, and was a teacher of social studies and science in Clearfield Central School in Newfield, NY. He enlisted in the army July 24, 1941 from Buffalo, NY. He graduated from officer's candidate school at Fort Benning, Georgia on May 19, 1942 and then served with the 81st Infantry Division. He married Janet Ellis on December 24th, 1943 at Camp San Louis Obispo, California. She was the daughter of Mr. and Mrs. W. Jay Ellis of Auburn, NY.

Captain Smith, was a regimental supply officer for the 322nd Infantry Regiment, was formerly a battalion supply officer and later company commander of service.

Capt. Smith was awarded the Soldier's Medal of heroism displayed during the American invasion of the Palau Island. The citation read, in part:

"Captain John H. Smith, 0-1284038, 322nd Infantry, United States Army, for heroism on Angaur Island, Palau Group, 30 September 1944. When enemy small arms fire ignited phosphorus grenades in an ammunition dump, fragmentation grenades and mortar shells stacked in the immediate vicinity became endangered by the flames, Capt. Smith, with complete disregard for his personal safety, seized the burning grenades and moved them from the immediate vicinity and in so doing received numerous burns about his body. The heroism displayed by Captain Smith saved government property from destruction and possible death or serious injury to the nearby troops"

He was killed in action on February 2, 1945 in the Philippines. His Chaplain wrote: "He was my most faithful attendant at all services." He was buried Woodlawn National Cemetery in Elmira, NY.

Survived by:
Wife: Janet or Janette Ellis of Auburn, NY.
Parents: Genevieve Smith and the late Edwin Smith of Delhi Rd. in Gainesville
Brothers: Edwin B. at Cornell University studying veterinary science; and Robert C., at home.
Sister: Frances S.

*Citizen Advertiser, Auburn, NY- January 3, 1944
*Castilian – March 1, 1945
*Gainesville News – February 1945
*Western New Yorker – February 15, 1945
*Wyoming County Times – January 11, 1945
*Military Record of the Town of Gainesville

Theodore Ernest Wagner

Pvt. 1st Class, U.S. Army

Theodore Ernest Wagner was born in Wayland, NY on August 28, 1924. He was baptized at Cohocton, NY on March 31, 1925. After a year in Cohocton his parents moved to Silver Springs, town of Gainesville. He was the captain of his school basketball team and graduated in the Silver Springs Class of 1942. He was a member of the Boy Scouts and attended the Methodist church. He was employed at Curtiss-Wright in Buffalo, NY. On Christmas Day of 1942 he became engaged to Jean Litteer who was a cadet nurse at the Wyoming County Community Hospital in Warsaw.

He entered the service in April 1943. From Fort Niagara, he went to Camp Mackall, NC, where he received his glider infantry training and

Camp Forrest, TN. During his training period in the states he won the following awards, Certificate of Qualified Gliderman on December 30, 1943 for having completed the prescribed course in knots and lashings, loading organizational equipment, safe loading principles and having made the prescribed number of glider flights and the Certificate as a Gas Non-Commissioned Officer, July 20, 1944. For having completed the prescribed course in the 17th Airborne Division Chemical Warfare School.

On September 19, 1944, he was chosen by his company to be decorated by the Colonel when those who had passed the Expert Infantry Test received their badges.

He went overseas and was stationed in England in August of 1944 until late December. He was then moved into France, then into Belgium where he gave his life at the age of 20 while in action at the Battle of Bastogne which was the beginning of the Battle of the Bulge of January 7, 1945. According to a letter received from his C.O. he was acting as First Scout for his company when hit by small gun fire and killed instantly.

He was buried at Grand Failly, France. In 1948 his body was returned from Europe for burial in Elmwood Cemetery in Silver Springs. He was awarded a Purple Heart and a Presidential Citation posthumously.

Survived by:
Fiancé: Jean Litteer of Warsaw, NY.
Parents: Ernest and Leola F. Wagner of Duncan Avenue in Silver Springs.
Grandmother: Mrs. Ione Flint of Cohocton, NY.

Perry Herald – December 11, 1948
Rochester Democrat and Chronicle – February 8, 1945
Silver Springs Signal – April 18, 1945
*Notebook of Stanley Rutherford, former Gainesville Historian
*Wyoming County Veterans Services Office

The Castilian newspaper, Castile, NY
January 9, 1941.

CHAPTER NINE

Genesee Falls

Leon E. Lathrop

Pvt. 1st Class
U.S. Marine Corps

Leon E. Lathrop was the first son of Adelbert and Laura Lathrop, born on May 5, 1920 in the town of Pike. The family moved between towns almost yearly and lived for a time in Gainesville and Castile as Adelbert was a tenant farmer. They later moved on a farm in Genesee Falls. After graduating from Castile High School in 1940, Leon attended Alfred University before enlisting in the Marines in February of 1942.

He trained at Parris Island and New Rider, NC where he left for overseas, arriving with the 1st Marines at Guadalcanal on August 5, 1942. He saw action in New Guinea, Cape Glousier and Peleliu Islands in the South Pacific where he was first reported as missing. The family received the telegram in November of 1944, only to later be notified that December that it was confirmed that Leon was killed in action on September 22nd. He was 24-years-old.

Leon had earned the Presidential Unit Citation Ribbon Bar with blue enameled star, the Asiatic-Pacific Campaign Medal and was posthumously awarded the Purple Heart.

This was the second son of Adelbert and Laura Lathrop to be killed during the war. The first, Robert S. Lathrop, was killed on September 8, 1944 (biography next).

Leon was originally interred in the Armed Forces Cemetery overseas in Grave 91, Row 7. In November of 1948, Leon and his brother Robert were brought back to the United States and taken to the Aldrich Funeral Home for services. They were buried in Grace Cemetery in Castile.

Survived by:
Parents: Adelbert H. and Laura (McLaughlin) Lathrop of Glen Iris Road in Castile, NY.
Brothers: Richard at home; the late Robert S. Lathrop, who was killed in action on September 8th.

The Castilian – January 18, 1945; April 19, 1945
Perry Herald – November 22, 1944; January 17, 1945
Wyoming County Times – November 14, 1948
Historical Wyoming, July 1975, pg. 19.

Robert S. Lathrop

Staff Sgt.
U.S. Army Air Forces

Robert S. Lathrop was the second of the sons born to Mr. and Mrs. Adelbert Lathrop on January 17, 1923. He graduated from Castile High School in 1942. He was active in athletics during his high school years. He was a varsity member of one championship basketball team that reached the semi-final round in the district sectional tournament. He entered the service shortly after graduating.

Sgt. Lathrop was a gunner on a B-24 Liberator Bomber and had completed more than 40 missions since arriving in the Mediterranean war theatre. He had been overseas since March and stationed with a heavy bomber squadron at an Italian base for the past several months. He had seen action over France, Italy, Germany, Austria, Hungary,

Rumania and Yugoslavia. He served with the 782nd Army Air Forces Bomber Squadron as a Staff Sergeant.

The War department stated that he was killed as a result of an accidental gunshot wound in Italy on September 8, 1944. His brother Pfc. Leon Lathrop was fighting with the Marines in the Pacific War Theater at the time of Robert's death at the age of 21. He would be the first of the Lathrop sons to give his life to their country. Fourteen days later, on September 22, 1944 his brother Leon would also be killed in action.

In November of 1948, Robert and his brother Leon were brought back to the United States to be buried in Grace Cemetery, Castile, NY.

His parents were presented with the Air Medal as well as the Distinguished Flying Cross on behalf of Robert.

After the flood of June 1972 destroyed the Genesee Falls town hall, a new one was built with federal disaster aid. On May 31, 1975, the hall was dedicated in honor of Leon and Robert Lathrop.

Survived by:
Parents: Adelbert H. and Laura Lathrop of Genesee Falls, NY.
Brothers: Richard resides with parents; Leon E. Lathrop was in service at the time.

*Perry Record – April 19, 1945; October 5, 1944; November 22, 1944; January 17, 1945
*Perry Herald – August 2, 1944
*Western New Yorker – November 23, 1944
*Castilian – September 28, 1944; October 5, 1944
*Unknown newspaper: April 11, 1946
*Wyoming County Times – November 4, 1948
*Wyoming County Veterans Services Office
*Certificate of Birth

Image from *The Torch*, Attica High School yearbook, 1944

CHAPTER TEN

Java

The town of Java historian, Mr. David Carlson, reports that no Java residents lost their life serving their country during World War II. There is also none listed in the *World War II Honor List of Dead and Missing, State of New York*, (War Dept. 1946)

Photograph by Nicholas Dovolos, son of George Dovolos of *The Sandwich Shop* est. 1932, (later known as *The Hole in the Wall* restaurant)—where every soldier was entitled to a free meal. From one of Nicholas' WWII albums, titled "Sicily 1943 to England 1944." Photo courtesy of Nicholas' son, George Dovolos, the third generation at the restaurant until 2001 when it was sold. The new owners still honor servicemen with a meal.

Perry Record, newspaper. May 6, 1943.

CHAPTER ELEVEN

Middlebury

Harold Quincy Bostian

Pvt. 1st Class, U.S. Army

Harold Quincy Bostian was born on March 17, 1924. A 1943 graduate of Wyoming Central School, he was well known as being one of the best-known basketball players in the area.

He entered the service in July 28, 1943 and trained at Camp Upton, NY then Camp Edwards, MA for 11 months. On May 6, 1944 he married Violet Carlson.

After spending Christmas at home he returned shortly thereafter to Fort Meade, MD. He left for overseas on December 28th to train briefly in England. From there he went to the war front on January 6, 1945 to serve with the U.S. Army Co. G, 318th Infantry Regiment, 80th Infantry Division.

He was first reported as missing in action since February 18, 1945. Word was received by the War Department, that he was killed in action in Luxembourg, Germany on February 19th. He was 20-yrs-old. Pvt. Bostian is buried at Luxembourg American Cemetery, Luxembourg City, Luxembourg, Plot H, Row 14, Grave 40. He was posthumously awarded the Purple Heart and Gold Star Buttons.

Survived by:
Wife: Violet (Carlson) Bostian of Middlebury.
Parents: Lawrence and Olive Rose (Blatchford) Bostian, 78 Main St., Wyoming Village in Middlebury.
Brother: Cpl. Robert Bostian, U.S. Army in France
Sisters: Mrs. Catherine Testa and Mrs. Eleanor Hoaker, both of Buffalo, NY; Mrs. Lucile Alexander of Perry, with husband in Army at Fort Sill, OK.
Maternal Grandmother: Mrs. Hattie Blatchford
Paternal Grandparents: Mr. and Mrs. Elmer Bostian of Milton, PA.

**Daily News,* Batavia, NY – March 5, 1945
**The Times,* Batavia – March 15, 1945
**Rochester Times Union* – April 3, 1945
*Wyoming County Veterans Services Office
*National WWII Memorial website

William S. Field

Pvt. U.S. Army

William S. Field of the village of Wyoming was born in Wellsboro, Pennsylvania on January 22, 1920.

William enlisted at Buffalo, NY on December 16, 1941 and was sent to Fort Niagara, NY on December 27th. From there Pvt. Field was sent to join the Air Corps at Keesler Field in Fort Biloxi, MS where he was a member of the 400 Technical School Squadron, Flight E.

He died on January 27, 1942 from drowning when the row boat he was in overturned in a squall on Black Bay in Biloxi. A memorial tree was dedicated at Wyoming Village Park in his honor.

The body was accompanied home by Private Milton Cassidy of Wyoming who had enlisted with William and gone to the Mississippi base together. Burial was in Wyoming Cemetery in Wyoming Village in the Town of Middlebury.

Survived by:
Parents: Homer and Catherine Field (Catherine remarries C. Francis Wright after Homer's death in 1952.)
Brother: Donald R. Field
Half-Brother: Archie Sweezy of Geneseo, NY.
Sister: June E. Field of Wyoming.
Grandmother: Mrs. Nettie Johns of Pavilion, NY.

Daily News, Batavia – January 29, 1942.
Wyoming County Times – February 5, 1942; June 19, 1952.
*Wyoming County Veterans Services Office.

(*NOTE: The correct spelling of his last name is Field not Fields, as is often times written in newspaper articles.)*

Richard Albert Rowe

1st Lt., U.S. Army Air Forces

Richard A. Rowe was born August 19, 1921. He was a graduate of Wyoming Central School, Class of 1938 and had been employed at the Haxton Canning Company at the time he entered the service in October 12, 1942.

Commissioned a 2nd Lt., he received his wings on August 13, 1943 from Luke Field, Phoenix, Arizona. He had spent a short leave at home in September 1943. The only leave he ever received during his training. In October 1943 he was sent to Hawaii where he was stationed for some time before being transferred to the South Pacific. He was a fighter pilot, serving in the 13th Air Force with the 68th Fighter Squadron as 1st Lt. He had completed 100 missions. In his last letter home dated January 23, 1945 he said he expected to be transferred back home for a visit in March.

JAMES GILLEN

On January 27, 1945, four days later, he was killed in an airplane accident on the Island of Leyte at the age of 23.

He was awarded the Following: The Air Medal "For meritorious achievement while participating in sustained combat operational missions as fighter pilot from 4 May to 10 May 1944." One Silver Oak-Leaf Cluster added to the Air Medal "For meritorious achievement while participating in sustained operational flight missions from 11 May 1944 to 1 June 1944; from 5 June 1944 to 11 June 1944; and from 18 August 1944 to 16 December 1944 in the Southwest Pacific Area during which hostile contact was probable and expected." One Bronze Oak-Leaf Cluster, representing six additional awards of the Air Medal which were awarded posthumously, "For meritorious achievement while participating in an aerial flight over Southeast Celebes, on 24 November 1944. Lieutenant Rowe, pilot of a P-38, participated in a fighter sweep to Kendari. Weather preventing an attack on his primary target, he searched along the Celebes coast for enemy shipping and spotted a freighter of 100 to 1500 tons tied to a 180 foot barge which appeared to be supplying it with provisions. His P-38 made several strafing passes, leaving the freighter in flames, the barge sinking, and at least six Japanese killed. The courage and devotion to duty displayed by Lieutenant Rowe are worthy of commendation."

During his memorial service in April of 1945, a silver plane high in the sky over the village of Wyoming was heartfelt by all who attended. He was buried in the Wyoming Cemetery in the village of Wyoming in Middlebury.

Survived by:
Parents: Dewey and Gertrude (Chase) Rowe of Wyoming.
Brothers: David and Keith, at home; Donald Rowe of Wyoming; P.F.C. Lester H. Rowe of the US Infantry, European Theater of Operations;

Pvt. Vernon Rowe, mechanic of the Air Corps at Buffalo and later training at Douglas Aircraft in Santa Monica, CA.
Sisters: Betty Rowe of Wyoming; Mrs. Thelma Randall of Perry Center, NY.
Grandmother: Mrs. Elizabeth Rowe

*Photograph of Richard Rowe featured on the cover of this book.
*Daily News, Batavia – August 2, 1944
*Perry Herald – March 7, 1945
*Western New Yorker – March 8, 1945; April 26, 1945
The Blast—Warsaw High School Yearbook, 1944.
Historical Wyoming– Vol. 48 Issue #3, January 2002 (Short biography.)
*Wyoming County Veterans Services Office

John A. Schadt

Paratrooper, Sgt., U. S. Army

John A. Schadt was one of seven children of George and Mayme Schadt. Originally from Buffalo, they moved to Wyoming County between 1930 and 1935. They lived on R.D. #1 in the village of Wyoming. John's parents moved to Warsaw sometime after 1940.

John was an employee of the Warsaw Elevator Company. He was married to Ethel E. Benson of Buffalo on November 29, 1941. John was 20-years-old when he enlisted on December 8, 1942 out of Buffalo. John's father, George, himself had registered for the draft on April 27, 1942 at the age of 54 at Local Board #571 in Warsaw.

In January of 1944 John was sent overseas to serve as a paratrooper for the 501st Parachute Infantry, 101st Airborne. He was originally listed as missing in action in Normandy, France on June 6th, D-Day. It was later confirmed he had been killed. He was posthumously awarded the Purple Heart. He is buried in St. Laurent (Permanent Cemetery) in St. Laurent, France in Block C, Row 13 Grave 17.

Survived by:
Wife: Ethel (Benson) Schadt of Buffalo, NY.
Parents: George and Mayme (Boltz) Schadt of 86 Linwood Avenue in Warsaw.
Brothers: Kenneth Schadt of Buffalo; Karl of Sloan, NY; and S 1C Frank Schadt serving in the Pacific.
Sisters: Emma, Lois and Velma (or Thelma) at home with her parents.

Buffalo Evening News: November 27, 1941; August 22, 1944.
Buffalo Courier Express: July 23, 1944; March 19, 1947.
*National WWII Memorial website

The Perry Record, newspaper. Thurs. May 13, 1943

CHAPTER TWELVE

Orangeville

The town of Orangeville historian, Laury Lakas, reports that no Orangeville residents lost their life serving their county during World War II. There is also none listed in the *World War II Honor List of Dead and Missing, State of New York*, (War Dept. 1946)

Photograph by Nicholas Dovolos from his WWII photo album titled "England 1943 to France 1944 to Home 1945." *Photo courtesy of his son, George Dovolos.*

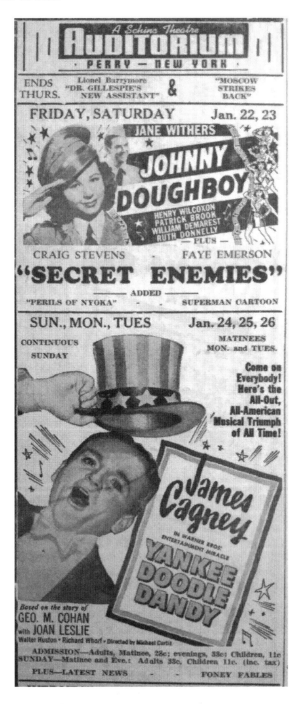

The Perry Record, newspaper. January 1943.

CHAPTER THIRTEEN

Perry

Charles R. Burgett

Staff Sgt., U.S. Army Air Forces

Charles R. Burgett was born in Perry on September 20, 1920. The family had resided on Leicester Street before moving with his parents to Andover, NY when he was five-years-old. Charles graduated from Andover High School in 1938.

On August 15th, 1942 he joined the Air Corps. He served as a Staff Sergeant and Asst. Radio Operator and gunner on B-17F, 416th Bomber Squadron, 99th Bomb Group.

When death came to Charles on October 1, 1943 in a Flying Fortress, somewhere on the European Front in  Switzerland, a second native of Perry, Lt. Donald Prentice, was also carried to his death in the same plane. They were members of the same crew, their aerial careers joining when the plane's crew was chosen at Gowen Field, Boise, Idaho. Both of these men had played together as children, however when stationed in Gowen Field they did not recognize each other until they talked about their hometowns.

The B-17F was attacked and shot down by enemy aircraft fire over Switzerland. Charles was the first man to be killed from Andover, NY.

In November, 1943 his family received the Purple Heart and Air Medal with five Oak Leaf Clusters award.

He was buried in Switzerland at the age of 23. On January 18th 1949 his body was brought back to the United States for burial in Hillside Cemetery in Andover, NY.

The Andover American Legion Post had changed its name to the Lynch-Burgett Post No. 397 to honor the first men from Andover to give their lives in the two World Wars—Thomas M. Lynch, World War I and Charles R. Burgett in World War II.

Survived by:
Parents: Ralph and Hazel Baker Burgett of Andover, NY.
Grandmother: Mrs. H. C. Burgett of Perry.

The Alfred Sun – January 20, 1949
Olean-Times Herald – October 12, 1943
Bolivar Breeze – November 14, 1946
Perry Herald – October 13, 1943
Rochester Times Union – October 13, 1943

Rodney Orlo DeMun

Pvt., U.S. Army

Rodney Orlo DeMun was born in Avoca, Steuben County, NY on January 15, 1920. He married Clara Dieter of Leicester, NY on January 2, 1939 at Mount Morris, NY.

Private DeMun first entered the service in February, 1942 but was discharged in December, 1942. He came home to Perry where his wife and children were living. He then worked briefly at the Kaustine Co. and The Borden Co in Perry.

On February 7, 1944, he was recalled and sent to Camp Swift, Texas, for training and was sent to Europe in September, 1944 where he served with the 306th Infantry Division in the 3rd Army on the German front. When he visited his home and family late in August he left a few personal effects, telling his wife, "If I go overseas I'll never return."

It was reported that he was missing in action on November 17, 1944, but later it was determined that he had met death at the age of 24, while fighting with the 3rd Army.

He was buried in Pleasant Valley Cemetery in the Hamlet of Piffard in the town of York, Livingston County, NY.

Survived by:
Wife: Mrs. Clara Dieter DeMun of 49 Bordon Ave. in Perry.
Children: Rodney Jr., Age 5; Sherman, age 2; Orlo, age 5 months.

Parents: Jay and Ada DeMun
Brothers: Roland DeMun of York, NY; Delbert DeMun of New Mexico
Sisters: Barbara and Rita, at home; Ruth Jones of Dansville, NY.

*Perry Herald – December 6, 1944
*Perry Record – December 7, 1944; December 21, 1944; December 16, 1948
**Rochester Times - Union* – December 19, 1944
*Wyoming County Veterans Services Office

Alton E. Dukelow

Pvt. 1st Class, U.S. Army

Alton E. Dukelow was born May 16, 1913 in Castile NY. The family later moved to Perry by 1922. He married Ada D. Smith on July 28, 1937 in Geneseo, NY. They lived for a time in Perry, had one child together, but would eventually divorce by August of 1944. Alton's parents later moved to a farm in Leicester, NY.

Alton entered the service on March 28, 1941 in Buffalo, NY and was stationed at Fort Niagara, then to Fort Eustis, Virginia with the 57th Coast Artillery. He was then sent to Camp Pendleton in Virginia.

In December of 1941 he was sent overseas and was stationed at the Schofield Barracks, Hawaiian Islands with the 180th Coast Artillery. He was fortunate to have a thirty day furlough to spend with his parents in Leicester at the end of April in 1944. A year later, on March 7, 1945, while his outfit was stationed in the South Pacific he was killed in action by a mine explosion on the Tinian Island in the Mariana Islands. He was brought back in June of 1948 on the B & O Railroad from Schenectady and arrived in Mt. Morris on the night of June 17th. A military funeral was conducted by the Perry American Legion Post. He was buried in Glenwood Cemetery in Perry.

Survived by:
Son: Alton Henry Dukelow (child with former wife, Ada, who would remarry).
Parents: James Dukelow and Lillian (Romasser) of Leicester, NY.
Brother: James Dukelow Jr. of Leicester, NY.
Sister: Mrs. Adelaide Stevens of Leicester, NY.

* *Wyoming County Times* - August 24, 1944.
**Livingston County Leader* (Geneseo) – June 16, 1948
*Perry Herald – June 17, 1948
*Wyoming County Veterans Services Office
*New York State Marriage Index, 1881-1967.

Leonard E. Emery

Sgt., U.S. Army

Leonard E. Emery was born in Perry on May 9, 1907. He was an ambitious young man as a child, mowing lawns and selling Sunday papers for Waldo Coburn. As an adult he was employed at the Perry Knitting Company.

He joined the U.S. Army in 1924 after his family left Perry. He served as a Sergeant in the 592nd Engineer Shore Regiment, U.S. Army. He was stationed on the Island fortress of Corregidor in the Philippines under General Douglas MacArthur until he was discharged in 1939 after 15 years of service and he returned to United States.

Shortly thereafter he volunteered as an enlisted U.S. citizen in the Royal Canadian Army. Observed to be a valuable asset to the Canadian Army, he was soon sent to England and then to France where he saw action against the Germans. All of this, taking place before his country and the U.S. had entered the war. In the spring of 1940 Sgt. Emery participated in one of the most significant events of the early conflict in Europe between Great Britain–France and its enemy the Germans under the tyrant dictator Adolph Hitler.

Sometime between May 27th and June 4th of 1940, Sgt. Emery was wounded by shrapnel during the massive troop evacuation at Dunkirk, France on the English Channel. In a small half circle (some say 15 miles) close to 350,000 English, French, and many British Common Wealth troops, such as the Royal Canadian Army to which Sgt. Emery was assigned, were bottled up by the Nazi Army and Air Force. Here at Dunkirk in early June 1940, was what was later called "The Deliverance at Dunkirk." Over a relatively short time period 338,226 troops were evacuated from France to England across the English Channel. Sgt. Emery, seriously wounded, was one of the 338,226 that made it to the safety of the English shore. Hundreds were killed, wounded and captured by the Germans.

While recovering from his wounds in an English Hospital he transferred back into the U.S. Army and sent back to United States. Here, for some months, he served as an instructor in Ranger tactics at Camp Edwards, MA. By now, the United States had entered the war. He was then sent to the South Pacific where he took part in U.S. Army action in Bougainville, the Admiralty, and Calabrese Islands. Finally, in the fall of 1944, he returned to the Philippine Islands where he had been 20 years before.

He was killed in action on October 25, 1944 on Leyte in the Philippines by the Japanese. He is buried at Manila American Cemetery and Memorial, Fort Bonifacio, Manila, Philippines.

Survived by:
Parents: Minnie Emery and the late Lemuel E. Emery
Brothers: Clarence; Philip Emery of Batavia; Herbert and William, both in the service.
Sisters: Mrs. Ethel Proctor of Rochester and a sister in Chicago, IL.

Rochester Times-Union – November 30, 1944
Perry Record - November 30, 1944
Perry Herald - November 29, 1944
*National WWII Memorial website

Edward Raymond Hall

Pvt., U.S. Army

Edward Raymond Hall was born May 18, 1913 at Royalton in Niagara County, NY and moved to Perry with his parents that same year. He was a 1930 graduate of Perry High School. He was employed at the Perry Knitting Company until April of 1941 until he left to take a course as a machinist at the Rochester Mechanics Institute and afterwards went to work for the Eastman Kodak Company.

A faithful member of the Presbyterian Church, he took an active part in young people's religious work and assisting as custodian of the building. He was a member of the Wyoming County Christian Endeavor Union. His interest in guns and marksmanship brought him into prominence as a member of the Perry Gun Club, charter member of the Commodore Rifle and Pistol Club and helped to organize the Junior Gun Club as an instructor.

Known as "Ray" in Perry, he enlisted on September 29, 1942 with the Army Ordnance Corps in Buffalo and reported for duty on October 6, 1942. Always interested in guns, he had waited until he could get into Ordinance because it was something in which he had a personal interest and talent that he felt would be of more use than any other branch. He was stationed at Fort Niagara, for three weeks before being sent to Aberdeen Proving Grounds in Maryland where he had finished his basic training and was attending "small arms school."

On Christmas Eve night of 1942 in Aberdeen, Edward and two of his friends—Vernon Clark of Denver, Colorado and Robert Carney of

Springfield, Massachusetts—were walking on the right side of the muddy road, with Hall nearest the center. They heard a truck approaching but paid no particular attention to it, as there was ample room for it to pass. The rain and hazy atmosphere obscured the driver's vision and he struck the three of them. Private Hall was killed instantly. Vernon received severe lacerations and an injured leg and recovered. Robert escaped uninjured. Mr. Carney was detailed to accompany the remains to Perry. He was the second Perry man to die while in service. He is buried at Glenwood Cemetery in Perry.

Survived by:
Parents: Edward and Ida Hall of Perry.
Brother: Robert Hall ~U.S. Army Camp Louis in Obispo, California
Sister: Audrey Hall, at home; Constance Hall of Dobbs Ferry, NY.

*Perry Herald – December 30, 1942
*Perry Record – December 31, 1942; June 1, 1944
*Wyoming County Veterans Services Office

Ward Samuel Hewitt

Pvt. 1st Class
U.S. Army

Ward Samuel Hewitt was born in LeRoy, NY on May 10, 1921. He moved to Silver Springs, NY and attended the Silver Springs High School. He was an employee of the Buffalo Arms Corporation in Buffalo where he resided prior to the war. He was married on May 8, 1940 to Frances Godfrey. Four children were born to them. Along with a large extended family, they claimed the Oatka Road, in Gainesville as their home.

He was inducted into the service on May 10, 1944 at Fort Dix, NJ, training chiefly at Fort Bragg and Camp Maxey, Texas. He went overseas in December of 1944 to serve in the European theater with Co. B, 22nd Reg., 4th Division, 3rd Army.

His two brothers were also in the service at the time of Ward's death, First Sergeant, LaVerne Hewitt, who was convalescing in a general hospital in Kentucky after completing 65 missions aboard a medium bomber. The other brother, Dean, was a seaman, 2nd class in the Navy, and was stationed in New York.

Ward was killed in action on March 2, 1945 in Germany at the age of 23. The body of Pfc. Ward S. Hewitt was returned home to be buried in Glenwood Cemetery in Perry.

Survived by:
Wife: Frances Arline (Godfrey) Hewitt of 79 Borden Ave., Perry. (Frances later remarried to David W. Roche.)
Sons: Robert, age 4; Ward Jr., age 2; and Leon, 2 ½ months.
Daughter: Joann, age 1.
Parents: Arthur and Blanche Hewitt of Oatka Rd. in Gainesville, NY.
Brothers: Corky "Irving" Hewitt, at home; and Sgt. Laverne "Jim" Hewitt, U.S. Army; S2ClL Dean Hewitt, U.S. Army.
Sisters: Mrs. Leo Beachel of Batavia, NY; and Mrs. Wallace Phillips of Covington Center, NY.
Grandparents: Mr. and Mrs. S. A. Oakes of Covington Center, NY; and Mr. and Mrs. Charles Hewitt of Oatka Rd.

*_Perry Herald_ – March 21, 1945
*_Perry Record_ – May 19, 1949
*Wyoming County Veterans Services Office

William Harvey Judd

Pvt. 1st Class
U. S. Army

William Harvey Judd was born in Perry on February 15, 1921. He enlisted on October 16, 1940 in Batavia, NY and was sent overseas on November 13, 1943. His records show that he had been wounded in action three times, one being February 13, 1945 in which he returned to action on February 15th since his injuries were not severe.

Ten days after returning to combat in Germany on February 25, 1945, he was killed in action while attached to Co. G 28th Infantry 8th Division in the European Theater.

He was buried at Henri Chapelle Cemetery, France. William's body was then returned in December 9, 1947 to be buried in Glenwood Cemetery in Perry.

Survived by:
Parents: Mattie Judd (and Noah H. Judd who died in 1942) of Perry who later moved to Warsaw.
Sisters: Twins Marie and Mae of Warsaw.

*Perry Record – March 28, 1945; December 18, 1947
**Daily News, Batavia* – November 25, 1947
*Perry Herald – December 11, 1947
*Wyoming County Veterans Services Office

Joseph Roger Knack

Pvt., U. S. Army

Joseph Roger Knack was born August 2, 1925. In his school life he was active in student affairs and played on both the football and track teams. He was known as one of the most popular members of his class. A graduate of Perry High School class of 1943, he became the editor of the school newspaper, *The Yellowjacket*, in his senior year. In his two years before graduation he worked at the *Perry Herald* where he was known as "Roge." According to his sister, his dream was to become a journalist. His family moved in 1943 after Joseph R.'s graduation. His father, who had been an employee of the Robeson Cutlery Co., took a job in Rochester.

After winning a scholarship to the Rochester Institute of Technology, Joseph R. studied printing where he obtained a job at Eastman Kodak in Rochester, NY.

He enlisted in December of 1943. Receiving his training at Camp Crowder, MO, in the Signal Corps, he was then sent overseas in August of 1944. While serving with 334th Infantry Regiment, the 84th Infantry Division on the German front on November 30, 1944, he was killed in action at the age of 19. He was buried in the Netherlands American Cemetery and Memorial in Margraten, Netherlands: Plot G, Row 16, Grave 23.

Survived by:
Parents: Joseph H. and Marie (Schmidt) Knack of 217 Pardee in Rochester, NY.
Sister: Doris Anne (Knack) Fyle

*Some listings have his name as J. Roger Knack, Joseph Roger Knack or Roger Knack.
Perry Herald – December 20, 1944
Rochester Times Union – December 18, 1944

Raymond Kolacinski

Pvt., U. S. Marine Corps

Raymond Kolacinski was born on December 19, 1920. He joined the service in January of 1942 and served with Company I, 5th Marines, 1st Marine Division.

Pvt. Kolacinski became the first Perry serviceman to be killed in action during World War II while he was serving with the U.S. Marines on Guadalcanal in the South Pacific. He was killed during enemy action on October 8, 1942 during the Solomon's Campaign.

His family was awarded the Purple Heart; the Presidential Unit Citation, which lists the battles in which the unit successfully participated; and an Asiatic-Pacific campaign medal, posthumously.

His body was returned in 1948 and arrived in San Francisco in February to continue on his final journey to Perry to be buried in St. Stanislaus Cemetery.

Survived by:
Parent: Benjamin Kolacinski of 65 Water St. and Mary (Piglowski) Kolacinski who was deceased.

Sisters: Violet Kolacinski (killed by an automobile in 1937); Mary Godlewski, 37 Water St., Perry; Mrs. Helen Szczepanowski .
Brothers: Anthony Kolacinski and Raymond's twin brother Henry Kolacinski, both of Perry; Benjamin Kolacinski of Chicago, Illinois. The following year brother Henry and Benjamin would serve with the Navy. Henry was in the South Pacific and Ensign "Benny" was with the Atlantic fleet on a destroyer.

*Perry Herald – August 18, 1943; February 12, 1948
*Perry Record – March 4, 1948

Alfred S. Kosciolek

Sgt., U. S. Army Air Forces

Alfred S. Kosciolek was born in Perry on January 27, 1922. The family lived at 173 Water Street until Alfred was about five years of age when the family moved to Buffalo, NY. His occupation was listed as a machinist.

He enlisted Army Air Corps on October 26, 1942 in Buffalo. He served as Sergeant and Gunner on B-24, 787th Bomber Squadron, 466th Bomber Group, Heavy.

A newspaper account stated he was on a flight from Brazil to Africa, but other sources say the flight was from the U.S. to Dakar in West Africa when their plane went down due to engine trouble at only 100 miles off the U.S. shore. According to their last radio message, they deployed the life rafts and were initially reported as Missing in Action. That was not to be the case. The crew of ten perished at sea on February 14, 1944. They are memorialized in the North Africa American Cemetery and Memorial in Tunisia on the Tablets of the Missing.

Survived by:
Parents: Joseph and Mary Angela Kosciolek of Buffalo, NY.
Sisters: Jane and Frances.

*Perry Herald – August 2, 1944
*Buffalo Courier Express – April 10, 1966.
*National WWII Memorial

Bennie (Benny) P. Marino

Pvt. 1st Class U. S. Army

Bennie P. Marino was born in Perry, NY in 1922. He had attended school in Perry, where the family resided until 1941 when they moved to Buffalo, NY. He was employed by the Bethlehem Steel Company before being inducted into the service.

On October 8, 1942 he enlisted in the Army at Buffalo and was sent overseas in March of 1943, as a Private First Class with the 794th Military Police Battalion.

Bennie was reported as missing in action in Italy on January 22, 1944. The telegram that arrived from the War Department was the first word they had that their son had been stationed in Italy. His death date was later declared as January 2, 1944, at the age of 22.

He is memorialized at Sicily-Rome American Cemetery and Memorial in Nettuno, Lazio, Italy. He was awarded the Purple Heart.

Survived by:
Parents: Mr. and Mrs. James Marino of 91 Schiller St. in Buffalo.
Brothers: Sgt. John Marino in the Army; Charles Marino, Coast Guard.

Perry Herald – February 6, 1944
Perry Record – February 17, 1944
Buffalo Evening News – February 14, 1944
*National WWII Memorial

Robert E. Mayhew

Cpl. T-5, U. S. Army

Robert E. Mayhew was born in 1910. He was a 1942 graduate of Perry High School. He had worked at the Silver Lake Golf Club near Perry for two years after he graduated. He resided in Monroe County, NY prior to the war. When he enlisted on July 7, 1942 he had been employed at Eastman Kodak Company in Rochester for five years.

He served as a signalman of the 350th Infantry, 88th Division in the Mediterranean Theater of the war. He had seen much action in 1944 during which the Allies had captured Sicily and were fighting a very strong German resistance when on September 28, 1944 was reported as missing in action. He was awarded the Infantryman's Badge for gallantry in action.

Since 1949 his remains were believed to have been buried in a military cemetery near Florence. Then, in 1960, a torrential mountain rain near Casola Valsenio in Northern Italy uncovered skeletal remains that were identified as Robert E. Mayhew's by his dog tags bearing his name and his next of kin, Maria, his wife. The United Press

International reported his body apparently lay buried for 15 years under a footpath in the Apennine Mountains until the rains caused a segment of the path to erode. The site is near Monte Battaglia (Battle Mountain), which was a stronghold for the German Gothic Line in the rugged area where some of the advancing United States 5th Army's fiercest battles took place in the late 1944 and early 1945. Additional identification included a rusted rifle, part of a bible, a gold bracelet, his wedding ring and a wrist watch. It had only been a year earlier that Robert's father had the Wyoming County Veteran's office write to the American Battle Monuments Commission to request a photo of his son's grave.

After the Army's Graves Registration Commission confirmed the finding, his parents agreed to have him buried in the Florence American Cemetery and Memorial in Florence, Italy.

At that time an Army spokesman said that the remains of the individual buried in 1949 in Florence, Italy with the mistaken identity of Cpl. Robert E. Mayhew would be studied by the Army Mortuary Service in an attempt to determine the true identity. We could find no information if that had been successful.

Survived by:
Wife: Mrs. Marie (Houghton) Mayhew of 56 S. Main St. in Perry. (Remarried Sept. 26, 1946 to Loren Wagner and resided in Pemberville, Ohio.)
Parents: Mr. and Mrs. Benjamin L. Mayhew of 20 Fruit St. in Perry.
Sister: Mrs. Luella Schumaker of Nunda, NY.

Nunda News – February 2, 1961
Perry Herald – January 26, 1961; February 2, 1961; October 18, 1941
*Wyoming County Veterans Services Office

Horatio "Ray" Migliore

Cpl., U. S. Army

Horatio Migliore was born December 18, 1910. He attended Mt. Morris High School and had worked for several years at the Perry Knitting Company in Perry. Later he held the position of radio repairman at the Davis Drug store. He was married Jan. 1, 1931 to Josephine Patanella of Mt. Morris, NY and they took up residence on Benedict Street in Perry village.

He enlisted in Erie, PA in May of 1942, being employed there at the time in a foundry. Horatio left for overseas duty sometime in the latter part of April, 1943. He served with the 180th Infantry Regiment, 45th Infantry Division.

In a letter to his wife in September, he had stated that he had, "captured 22 Germans." A telegram in which he said he was well came shortly after the letter. She had only just recently received a package with linen table cloths and napkins made in Milan and a ring. It was only a short time later his wife received the telegram of his death. He was in action against German forces in Italy when on October 12, 1943 he was killed in the Battle of Salerno.

He is buried in the Sicily-Rome American Cemetery in Nettuno, Italy: Plot J Row 3, Grave 58.

Survived by:
Wife: Josephine (Patanella) Migliore of 11 Benedict St. Perry. (She later moved to Harbor Walk in Buffalo, NY.)
Children: John Migliore, aged 10; Anna Mary, age 5
Father: John Migliore of Mill St. in Mt. Morris, NY.
Brothers: Pfc. Samuel Migliore, stationed with Army in the Pacific; App. Seaman Anthony Migliore; Pvt. Angelo Migliore in England with the US Army; Petty Officer Louis Migliore, US Navy, in Bainbridge, MD.
Sisters: Francis Proyo of Mt. Morris; Josephine Cipolio of Rochester, NY.

*_Perry Herald_ – November 10, 1943
*_Perry Record_ – December 16, 1943
*National WWII Memorial
*Wyoming County Veteran's Services Office

Thomas Arthur Parker Jr.

Staff Sgt., U. S. Army

Thomas Arthur Parker Jr. was born on January 30, 1918 in Rochester NY, coming to Perry in 1928. He had attended Castile District School No. 5 and later Perry High School. He was employed at Perry Knitting Mill and was engaged in farming with his father.

He enlisted in the Army in October 11, 1940 at Batavia, NY prior to the outbreak of the war. Thomas received his basic training at Fort Slocum and was assigned to duty in California. He was stationed in Hawaii at Pearl Harbor when on December 7, 1941 the Japanese attacked the United States.

After Pearl Harbor he was moved into the South Pacific and saw action as a member of the Co. D 35th Infantry and 25th Division. He was in the battles for Guadalcanal, Vella LaVella, Russell Islands, in the Solomon Islands, and New Caledonia—all in the South Pacific. He had also served in New Zealand but had not been in action there.

Sgt. Parker received the Combat Infantryman badge, American Defense ribbon, the Asiatic-Pacific ribbon with two Battle Stars, several Bronze Stars and the Good Conduct ribbon.

He was killed in action on March 27, 1945, at age 27, on Luzon Island in the Philippines. He was awarded the Purple Heart, posthumously. His body returned home on the B & O Railroad at 7:50 p.m. on Thursday, August 26, 1948. The body was escorted to Eaton's (now Eaton Watson) funeral home by the American Legion and VFW of Perry with burial that Saturday in Glenwood Cemetery in Perry.

Survived by:
Parents: Thomas and Alberta Parker of N. Center St. in Perry.
Brothers: Irving W. Parker, with Patton's Third Army in Germany; Carl E. Parker was discharged after being wounded at Anzio in Italy.

Perry Record – April 26, 1945; August 26, 1948; October 5, 1944
Perry Herald –April 25, 1945
*Wyoming County Veterans Services Office

Donald Morrow Prentice

1st Lt., U. S. Army Air Forces

Donald Morrow Prentice was born on December 7, 1917 in Perry, the only child of Ella and Herman Prentice. He graduated 4th in his class from Perry High School in 1934. While in high school he played varsity football as a guard and was center on the basketball team. Before entering the service he was employed at Robeson Cutlery Company.

He was a member of Troop I 101st Cavalry National Guard in Geneseo, NY for many years when he was inducted in January 27, 1941 and left for Fort Devens, MA.

He was then selected for air training at Ellington Field, Texas in January 1942, where after much training he earned his pilot wings and commission as 2nd Lieutenant in January, 1943. He was later promoted to First Lieutenant. He had been flying twin engine planes at Ellington. He was trained at several flying fields, notably Gowen Field, Idaho. Donald was shipped overseas in May, 1943 to serve with the 416th Bomber Squadron, 99th Bomb Group.

On a mission as pilot of a Flying Fortress on October 1, 1943, over Germany his plane was attacked, damaged and crashed on Switzerland soil, where he was killed along with another Perry native, Charles Burgett. Their aerial careers began when the plane's crew was chosen at Gowen Field, Boise, Idaho. Both of these men had played together as children, however when stationed in Gowen Field they did not recognize each other until two weeks later when they talked about their hometowns.

A week before his death a letter was sent to his family saying he had been flying extensively over Sicily, Italy and France, and described his experience as "very nerve wracking." He also said, "It would be nice to come back after the war and go over the same territory as a tourist."

He was buried with full military honors in Switzerland. His maternal grandfather Henry Reace was born in Berne, Switzerland where relatives still lived. In 1948 remains of 4,384 American soldiers who were buried in other countries were brought back to the United States aboard the U. S. Army Transport Barney Kirschbaum for burial, among them was Donald M. Prentice who was then buried in Glenwood Cemetery in Perry.

Survived by:
Parents: Herman C. and Ella C. Prentice of 35 Borden Ave. in Perry.
Sister: Mrs. Shirley (Mahron) Corbett of Syracuse, NY.

Buffalo Courier Express – December 28, 1948
Perry Herald – October 6, 1943; October 1, 1944; October 21, 1943; Jan. 20, 1943
*Wyoming County Veterans Services Office

PERRY HERALD, PERRY, N. Y., WEDNESDAY, JANUARY 27, 1943

Precision is the watchword with the pilots of these twin-engine AT-9 training planes, caught by the camera in a formation flight over the Army Advanced Flying School at Lubbock, Texas. The pilots are among those who received their silver wings in class 43-A and are "ready and rarin' to go" to join their comrades in spreading aerial death and destruction to the Axis. These are the type planes Lieut. Donald M. Prentice of Perry was flying at the time he received his commission and Wings a few days ago at Ellington Field.

Lawrence E. Rider

Staff Sgt., U. S. Army Air Forces

Lawrence E. Rider was born in Perry, NY on November 30, 1919. He had attended Perry High School. He was employed on farms and at the Perry Knitting Company.

He had entered the service on February 25, 1942 at Warsaw. He trained successively at Camp Lee, VA; Elgin Field, FL; Columbia, SC Army Air Base; and DeRidder Field in LA.

When he trained at Camp Lee, he was assigned to the medical corps and when volunteers were sought for gunners for bombing planes, he volunteered and was sent to Drew Field, Louisiana. He received advanced training at Charleston, SC and DeRidder, LA. He was then sent to North Africa as a gunner in February of 1943, with the rank of Staff Sergeant.

He made national news when the press associations carried a story of his aerial encounter in which he gunned down a Nazi plane over Tunisia. It was his first and occurred on April 14th, shortly after he landed in North Africa. He was part of several bombing operations over Sicily, which made the Allied invasion of that island possible. He had been a crew member of a B-26 medium bomber, one of the fastest of the lot.

On July 3, 1943, he wrote a letter to his friends on the *Perry Herald* staff, "I sure have had some very exciting experiences here and probably will have more before it is over."

On July 5, 1943 while serving in the North Africa-Sicily campaign he was reported missing in action over Sicily and presumed dead. The plane took a direct hit by the enemy and all five crew members were killed along with the pilot's little dog Scrappy. He was officially declared dead a year later by the War Department. They are buried or memorialized together at Zachary Taylor National Cemetery in Louisville, Jefferson County, Kentucky in Section E, Plot 246.

Survived by:
Mother: Mrs. Laura (Tuttle) Rider (wife of the late William Rider) of 53 St. Helena St. in Perry.
Brothers: Donald Rider, at home; Harold Rider, U. S. Army.
Sisters: Thelma, age 25; Lois, age 17; Jane, age 12.

*Perry Herald – August 4, 1943; August 2, 1944
*Perry Record - August 5, 1943
*Wyoming County Veterans Services Office

Richard N. Spellicy

Staff Sgt., U. S. Army

Richard N. Spellicy was born in Perry, NY. July 21, 1920. He was a 1937 graduate of Perry High School. He had attended Ohio State College for two years, where he studied business administration and majored in accounting, before entering the service in July 1942. He was employed by the A & P store, the Perry Knitting Co. and a member of Perry Methodist Church.

He was inducted in July of 1942 being stationed at Camp Gruber and Fort Sill, both in Oklahoma; Camp Polk, LA; and Camp Sam Houston in Texas. He was sent overseas in December, 1943, serving along with about seven other Perry soldiers, with Lt. General Mark Clarks 5th Army, 88th Blue Devils Infantry Division-338th Field Artillery in Italy. The other Perry soldiers in this unit were Robert Mayhew, Harry Schwartz, Sam Castiglia, Jack Hallows, Walter Tarala, Tony Tortorice, and Henry Thayer. He also was with the famous American Fifth Army which had pushed ahead in Italy after capturing Rome.

Sgt. Spellicy wrote about his duties in April, 1944. "My job is primarily directing fire from O.P.'s so I get my war first hand. It gets rough at times but all you need is common sense and good faith to pull you thru."

He was killed in action in Italy on July 17, 1944 while seeking cover in a farm house from German artillery fire. A shell killed him and injured a lieutenant. The lieutenant made it back to camp and told the Capt. O'Hara. The Captain went back himself to recover Sgt. Spellicy's body. He was buried in Florence American Cemetery, Via Cassia, Italy Plot A, Row 12, Grave 36.

Survived by:
Parents: Roy A. and Mabel Spellicy of Perry.
Brothers: Pat at home; Dr. Jack Spellicy of Rochester, NY.

Perry Herald – August 2, 1944
Perry Record – November 30, 1944; Dec. 2, 1944; August 3, 1944; August 9, 1945
*Wyoming County Veterans Services Office
*National WWII Memorial
*A more detailed account can be found in the October 2018 issue, Vol. 65 Issue #4, of *Historical Wyoming*.

Perry Record newspaper. May 13, 1943.

Michael Surtel

Cpl., U. S. Army

Michael Surtel was born February 13, 1916 in Perry, NY and had attended Perry High School. He was an employee of the Perry Knitting Company.

He entered the service in July, 1941 he had spent two years in the United States at various training camps. In a letter which appeared in the *Perry Herald* on June 9, 1943 reads:

"I've been in the army 23 months and so far have been in eleven camps. In all that time I have met just one Perry fellow at Camp Johnston, Lawrence Jacuzzo by name.... Last time I heard from my brother (Joseph) was when I was on my furlough in Perry in May. He is still in Indio, Cal., or vicinity I believe."

In 1943 Pvt. Surtel was sent overseas to England. He was a member of early invasion forces on the French Coast. He served with the 112th Infantry, 28th Division.

Pvt. Michael Surtel was killed in action in France on August 1st, 1944. He was the first soldier to be killed in France from Perry. His mother had a premonition something was wrong and stayed home from church on Sunday the 27th, when she received notice from the War Department.

His body arrived home on the B & O Railroad on September 24,1948, escorted by the Honor Guard of the American Legion and VFW to the Eaton[-Watson] Funeral home in Perry. Services were conducted the next day at St. Stanislaus Church with full military honors and burial in St. Stanislaus Cemetery in Perry.

Survived by:
Parents: Julia (Rudyk) Surtel and the late John Surtel of 135 Water St. in Perry.
Brothers: Stephen Surtel, U. S. Navy; Joseph Surtel, U. S. Army.

Perry Herald – June 9, 1943; August 30, 1944; August 26, 1948; September 28, 1948
Perry Record – September 7, 1944; August 31, 1944
Rochester Times-Union – August 29, 1944
*Wyoming County Veterans Services Office

Anthony J. Tortorice Jr.

Tech 4th Grade
U. S. Army

Anthony J. Tortorice Jr. was born in Perry, NY on December 26, 1920. He was an employee of the Perry Knitting Company. He then became a member of the Civilian Conservation Corp stationed at Letchworth State Park and in Schenectady. As a member of the CCC he had been an outstanding amateur boxer. Upon leaving the CCC in 1938 he went to work for the Dovolos Sandwich Shop.

Anthony entered the service on July 17, 1942 and stationed at Camp Gruber, Oklahoma. He continued his amateur boxing while in the military and had won 86 out of 90 bouts he had fought.

On December 1, 1943 he was sent overseas as cook for the 351st Infantry, 88th Division. "Tony" as he was called was ranked as a cook, but had participated in combat as his division progressed toward the occupation of Italy when every man was needed. He had proudly taken part in the triumphal Army parade through Rome after the city was captured. He had escorted a mule train, laden with supplies, over the mountains of Italy to American positions. On one patrol duty they came across a cave in which 150 men and women had been hiding for the past seven months.

Pvt. Thomas Nardoci of Perry, in a letter home, told of visiting Tortorice on September 21, 1944 and found him asleep under a straw stack. They talked for three hours after that. Pvt. Nardoci was with the 85th Division and a mere three miles from Tortorice's 88th Division unit.

Anthony was wounded in action in Italy three days later and died the same day from the wounds he received. He was originally interred in Italy. In 1948, Anthony was brought back to the United States aboard the Army Transport Lawrence Victory for re-burial at St. Joseph's Cemetery in Perry.

Survived by:
Parents: Anthony and Eleanora Tortorice of 28 Walnut Street, and later 50 Pine St. in Perry.
Brothers: Raymond and Nunzio.
Sisters: Eleanor, Josephine, and Mary

*Perry Record – October 19, 1944; November 4, 1948
*Perry Herald – October 11, 1944; October 18, 1944; November 1, 1944; November 11, 1948; November 18, 1948
*The Daily News – November 8, 1948
*Wyoming County Veterans Services Office

Herbert C. Trace

Pvt., U. S. Army

Herbert C. Trace was born November 25, 1905. In 1938 he came to Warsaw and worked as a chef for two years at the Watkin's Hotel. In 1940 he purchased the Koffee Kitchen Restaurant on Covington Street in Perry from Fred Schofield and operated it for one year. After he sold the Perry location he was a chef at Schwelzer's Diner in Avon and Geneva. He maintained his residence in Wyoming County. On November 5, 1942 he went to Buffalo to enlist in the army.

He died suddenly of a heart attack on the afternoon of November 13, 1942 at Fort Niagara—less than twenty-four hours after he reported for duty. His funeral was held at Port Huron, his former home, with burial in Linwood Cemetery in Sanilac County, Michigan.

*Perry Herald - November 18, 1942; December 14, 1950
*Wyoming County Times – November 19, 1942
*Avon Herald News – November 20, 1942

CHAPTER FOURTEEN

Pike

Theodore William Hunt

Pvt. 1st Class
U. S. Marine Corps

Theodore William Hunt was born November 17, 1923 and attended Pike Seminary when he lived with his family in Pike. During his high school days he lived with an uncle and aunt, Mr. and Mrs. E. C. Chaffee in Rochester, NY where he had attended and graduated from Madison High School in 1941. He was attending college in Rochester and planned to take a college course in aeronautical engineering but decided to enlist in the service. He was a member of the Senior High Department of Westminster Presbyterian church.

He attempted to enlist in the Marine Corps the week of the Pearl Harbor attack but had to have a nasal operation before he was accepted. On January 8, 1942 he enlisted in the Marine Corps and left Buffalo for Parris Island, SC where he completed his training, earning medals for marksmanship in both pistols and rifle. Pvt. Hunt was transferred to New River, NC where he was placed in Co. I, 3rd Branch, 7th Regiment, Fleet Marine Force, a company that had already been training for a year. Three months later Pvt. Hunt, along with his unit, sailed from the San Diego, California Marine Base for the South Pacific where he spent about six weeks on a ship.

During the Guadalcanal Campaign he was wounded in the leg by shrapnel and removed to a hospital in New Zealand to recuperate from the wound and malaria. In February, 1943 he rejoined the First Marine Division in Australia where he was awarded the Purple Heart. A few days before Christmas his family received a letter from him that he was back in the troop and eager to get into action.

In February of 1944 his father was informed by the Captain under whom his son had served, that his son was hit twice by rifle fire but kept on working his gun until hit a third time and killed. He died on December 26, 1943 in the South Pacific during the Invasion of Cape Gloucester. Mr. Hunt also received a letter from three of his son's buddies who said that what his son accomplished enabled them to advance and annihilate the enemy.

On February 16, 1949, Pvt. Hunt was laid to rest at the Veterans Plot in Pike Cemetery. He was the first soldier from the town of Pike to give his life. The Hunt-Stout Post in Pike is named after Grant G. Stout and Theodore William Hunt.

Survived by:
Parents: Mr. and Mrs. Charles Hunt; Pike, NY.
Sister: Wilma June Hunt (age 14); Pike, NY.
Uncle and Aunt: Mr. and Mrs. E. C. Chaffee; Rochester, NY.
Grandfather: William Davies

*Perry Herald – February 8, 1944, February 16, 1944, February 18, 1944 June 16, 1944
*Arcade Herald - August 7, 1942
*Rochester Times Union – February 5, 1944, February 19, 1944
*The Castilian – January 15, 1942; February 17, 1944; March 3, 1949
*Wyoming County Times – December 26, 1943; February 24, 1944
*Wyoming County Veterans Services Office

Grant Gates Stout

1st Lt., U. S. Army Air Forces

Grant Gates Stout was born on November 26, 1922 in Pike, NY. He was a 1941 graduate of Pike Seminary High School class of 1941 and a member of the Pike Presbyterian Church.

He enlisted in the Air Corp on January 12, 1943 and trained at the South East Area Training Command at Maxwell Field in Alabama. He was commissioned as a pilot on November 3rd that same year at Spence Field, Georgia. He was stationed next at Richmond, VA Air base as flying commander and instrument pilot instructor. He was sent overseas to the European Theater of operations with the 9th Air Force in April 1944.

In an interesting twist, while driving the perimeter of the Ninth Air Force fighter base, 1st Lt. Stout of Pike spotted something he recognized at a farmhouse he passed. He turned his jeep around and went back. There beside the house was a burned up German truck surrounded by craters left by the bombs he had dropped on D-Day.

On March 19, 1945 during an allied air raid over Brakel, Germany his plane was shot down. Lt. Stout was able to parachute safety out and landed near Dortmund, Germany. He was captured by a German soldier who turned him over to German civilians who then beat him severely. In an attempt to run away from this torture, he was shot and killed by the very same German soldier that had originally captured him.

A trial was held against the German soldiers responsible for his death. It is noted that they walked the flyer toward the air raid shelter where they met the commanding officer. A large crowd of civilians were on their way to the shelter at the time. A German soldier incited the crowd to beat and kill the flyer under the threat of being denied the use of the shelter. Brutally beatings from the German soldiers also occurred at the same time using clubs, stones and garden implements. Post war crime trials proved these facts.

He was found buried in an isolated grave near Dortmund, Germany and was later reburied in the United States Military Cemetery, in Belgium and then in 1949 returned to Pike for burial at Pike Cemetery. His headstone reads 1st Lieut., 387 AAF Fighter Sq. He received the Distinguished Flying Cross and Air Medal with 14 Oak Leaf Clusters.

Survived by:
Parents: Merle and Mabelle Marcille Stout of Pike, NY.
Sisters: Lyla K. Stout of Rochester, NY: and Mrs. John R. Trout, Yba City, CA.

*The Castilian – March 20, 1947
**Rochester Democrat and Chronicle* – June 8, 1949
*Unknown paper – September 22, 1944
**United States v. Georg Mayer et al.*, trial document at Wyoming County Historian's office

Eugene Robert Youngberg

Seaman 1st Class
U. S. Navy

Eugene Robert Youngberg was born on May 4, 1921 in Elma, NY. He attended School 52 and later McKinley Vocational High School in Buffalo, NY and majored in horticulture. Although working for the American Magnesium Co., his life's calling was to become a Lutheran Faith minister, an ambition he would have attained had he not been killed.

He joined the United States Navy at the age of 20 on July 12, 1942. He was a crew member aboard a destroyer, the *USS Nicholson* that made several trips across the Atlantic on convoy duty. The *Nicholson* was involved, along with many other allied ships, in the invasions of Casa Blanca, Sicily and Italy. After the Anzio Beach Invasion in Italy, the ship was sent back to the New York Navy Yard for repairs and then on to the South Pacific to join the 3rd Fleet under Admiral Bull Halsey. The destroyer was assigned the task of roaming the seas from Japan, Okinawa, Formosa, and the Philippines on neutralization raids and on the prowl for the Japanese Navy.

The *USS Nicholson's* outstanding contribution to the campaign came when she was ordered to proceed to the entrance of Seeadler Harbor in an attempt to draw fire from batteries known to be hidden there. The *Nicholson* commenced rifling runs at the Hauwei Island, decreasing their range at each firing. When at 750 yard range, shells were fired by the Japanese in rapid succession. One hit No. 2 gun mount upper handling room on March 6, 1944 killing three men and wounding four seriously. One of the three killed was Eugene Robert Youngberg.

He had participated in many battles in both the Atlantic and Pacific areas and received stars for seven major actions.

He was originally buried on Las Negros Island. Two years later his body was removed to New Guinea. From there the remains were brought to the land of his birth. On February 16, 1949, a double military funeral was held for Seaman Youngberg, along with a fellow Pike serviceman PFC Theodore Hunt where they were finally laid to rest in Pike Cemetery.

Survived by:
Parents: Erik A. and Helena A. Youngberg of Pike.
Brothers: Erik A. Youngberg, Lt. in Navy; Lloyd B. Youngberg, Electrician's Mate 2nd Class, Seabees
Sisters: Gloria J. Youngberg, Mrs. Alfred J. Pitzel and Mrs. Robert Miller.

Note to Reader: Seaman Youngberg's parents were both born in Finland. They immigrated to Canada and were married at Windsor, Ontario before moving to Buffalo and later to the town of Pike.

Western New Yorker – March 3, 1949; March 9, 1944
Unknown paper – February 24, 1949
The Castilian – March 3, 1949

Wyoming County Times, newspaper. March 9, 1944

The Perry Herald, newspaper. October 14, 1943.

CHAPTER FIFTEEN

Sheldon

Leon W. George
Sgt., U. S. Army

Leon W. George was born December 13, 1914 in Johnsonburg, a hamlet of Sheldon. He was a member of St. Cecelia's R. C. Church at Sheldon. He was one of the first Selective Service groups to go from Wyoming County on January 10, 1941.

Sgt. George left for the European Theater of Operation in October 1942. A sergeant in the 67th Regiment 2nd Armored Division he saw action in the African and Tunisian campaigns, returning to England after the capture of Tunisia. On July 5, 1944 his regiment was sent to France. He had hoped to see his brother, Francis Willis George, who was stationed in France whom he hadn't seen for three years, however, they were unable to connect. On July 15, 1944 he was killed in action at the age of 29.

Leon W. George was buried in Normandy American Cemetery, France in Plot G, Row 14, Grave 22. A memorial service was conducted at St. Cecelia's Church on August 3rd. He was posthumously awarded the Purple Heart.

Survived by:
Parents: Mrs. Julia R. (Graff) George of Johnsonburg and the late Joseph H. George.
Brothers: Norbert; Carl; Darwin; Vincent; Nelson, Flight Officer, U.S. Air Corp; Francis Willis, U.S. Army France; and one brother Clarence who preceded Leon in death.
Sister: Mrs. Edith Stoll of East Aurora.

*The Attica News – August 3, 1944; September 28, 1944
The Batavia Daily – August 9, 1944
**Western New Yorker* – August 10, 1944
*Wyoming County Veterans Services Office

Richard Francis Laird

Carpenter's Mate
U. S. Navy

Richard Francis Laird was born in the hamlet of Varysburg, town of Sheldon on May 23, 1922, the son of David and Nellie Laird. He later resided for many years with his grandparents, Mr. and Mrs. Edwin Glor of Varysburg. He attended school in Varysburg and enlisted in the Navy as soon as he was old enough. He was locally known as "Skee" Laird.

In 1941 he was serving as a crewman aboard the aircraft carrier *USS Hornet* and had participated in the Jimmy Doolittle bombing raid of Tokyo, Japan. His ship, the *USS Hornet*, was sunk in the South Pacific. Richard survived his ship's sinking and was assigned to the *USS Princeton*, also an aircraft carrier. Most of the newspaper clippings have him as Carpenter's Mate 1st Class or Carpenter's Mate 2nd Class. Online however, it states he was a Gunner's Mate. (There may be some confusion as there was another Richard Francis Laird, who was from Seattle, WA that is listed as Gunner's Mate 2nd Class.)

The *Princeton* later became engaged against the Japanese in a great naval battle off the Philippines. The *Princeton* was very severely damaged on October 24, 1944 when the Navy inflicted a crushing defeat to a Japanese armada bent on sealing off Gen. MacArthur's men on Leyte, shortly after the invasion of the Philippines began. Survivors were transferred to adjacent U.S. Navy vessels and the *Princeton* was sent to the bottom by American warships. On that day, Richard F. Laird was declared missing in action. In January of 1945, his Aunt Ruth Steele of Attica received official word from the Navy that he was considered dead. Early reports stated that 1,360 men survived the sinking; sadly, Petty Officer Laird was one of the 140 sailors who lost their lives in this battle.

He is memorialized at Manila American Cemetery and Memorial on the Tablets of the Missing at Fort Bonifacio, Manila, Philippines. There is also a headstone at Pleasant View Cemetery, Dutch Flats in Orangeville for his memory. He was the recipient of a Purple Heart and the Navy Specially Meritorious Medal, posthumously.

Survived by:
Brother: Vernon, U.S. Army
Half Brother: Willard
Aunt: Mrs. Ruth Steele of Attica, NY.
Grandparents: Mr. and Mrs. Edwin Glor

*Attica News – January 21, 1943; November 16, 1944; January 18, 1945
*National WWII Memorial

USS *Hornet* (1941)
Collection of Naval History and Heritage Command.

John Edward Maher

Sgt., U. S. Marine Corps

John Edward Maher was born on February 1, 1917 in Pike, NY. He was a graduate of Pike Seminary. He graduated from Alfred University School of Agriculture on April 3, 1934. He had been employed as a truck driver for B.J. Fisher of Warsaw, NY.

He enlisted on May 19, 1941 at Syracuse, NY and left for his basic training at Parris Island, SC. After completing basic training in August of 1941 he was assigned to guard duty at Brooklyn Navy Yard and at the Navy Building in Washington, DC. In September of 1943, he was transferred to Camp Lejeune, NC and from there he was sent overseas where he served on New Caledonia, Russell and Peleliu Islands with 7th Marines, 1st Marine Division.

He was killed in action on September 19, 1944 while fighting on Peleliu Islands in the South Pacific.

He was awarded the American Defense Medal, Asiatic-Pacific Campaign Medal and Purple Heart. His body was recovered and originally buried in the National Cemetery in Pelelieu. A memorial mass was held on May 20, 1945 at St. Joseph's Church in Varysburg. On November 10, 1948, his remains were returned from the Pacific for burial in St. Michael's Cemetery in Warsaw.

Survived by:
Parents: Edward T. and Kathryn R. Maher of Varysburg, NY.
Sisters: Mrs. Mary Eddy of Buffalo, NY; Mrs. Nora Billings of Corfu, NY; Mrs. Rita Rooney and Mrs. Eileen Rooney both of Castile, NY.

*Batavia Daily News – December 7, 1945
*Western New Yorker – January 4, 1945; May 24, 1945
*Perry Herald & Silver Springs Signal – November 11, 1948
*Wyoming County Veterans Services Office
*Alfred University, Archivist

CHAPTER SIXTEEN

Warsaw

William H. Atwell

Pvt., U. S. Army

William H. Atwell was born in Willowvale, NY on November 27, 1924. William attended Warsaw High School until 1941 and was an accomplished athlete active in football, basketball, baseball and bowling. For two years he held the local tennis championship.

On February 23, 1943 he was inducted into the Army and was sent overseas to the South Pacific in March of 1944. He served with 305th Infantry Regiment, 77th Infantry Division.

On August 7, 1944 he had volunteered to assist the U. S. Marine Corp as a Corpsman during the Battle of Guam and was killed.

In February, 1945 his parents were presented with the Bronze Star by Captain Charles M. Scott, Jr. the Personal Affairs Officer of the Western New York Military District, who was designated by Col. John M. McDowell, Commanding officer of District No. 4, 2nd Service Command at Buffalo, NY. The Bronze Star Citation reads:

"For heroic achievement in connection with military operations against the enemy. Private Atwell and another litter bearer became separated from a patrol, of which they were volunteer members, amid thick woods. They had just shot and probably killed a Japanese soldier who had attacked them with a grenade. The patrol as a whole, and they in particular had been assigned the mission of recovering the body of a slain comrade. So great was Private Atwell's devotion to duty that, despite his non-combatant status and without regard for personal risk, he and his companion undertook a local reconnaissance to see, if the trail was clear so they could proceed with the removal of the body. While so engaged, Private Atwell was shot in the face and apparently killed instantly."

Pvt. William Atwell is today memorialized in the Courts of the Missing at the National Cemetery, Oahu, Hawaii. The cemetery is known as the "Punchbowl," as its shape is formed as an old volcano.

Survived by:
Parents: William and Alice Atwell of 11 Brooklyn St. in Warsaw.
Sister: Mrs. William Blatchford of Warsaw.

Western New Yorker – September 14, 1944
Rochester Times Union – September 19, 1944
Wyoming County Times – February 22, 1945; August 9, 1945
* National WWII Memorial website

Note to Reader: A 2003 story entitled "The Last Letter Home," written by the author, appeared in Vol. 50, Issue #2 of *Historical Wyoming* and provides more information about Pvt. Atwell's life.

Frank Kenneth Barnes

Seaman, 2nd Class
U. S. Navy

Frank Kenneth Barnes was born on January 19, 1922 in Cincinnati, Ohio. He lived with his brother Edward on Baker-Banton Road in Warsaw after the death of their father in 1933. According to Frank's sister Arlie, Frank worked on several farms in Batavia before he enlisted in 1941. He trained at the Newport, Rhode Island Naval Training Station.

A message from the Navy Department to Edward Barnes, said he was unaccounted for when the *USS Sims*, a destroyer, was lost during a five day battle north of Australia that began on May 4, 1942. Seaman Barnes thus became the first Town of Warsaw serviceman to be killed in action in World War II.

The U. S. Navy destroyer that he served aboard was engaged with the Japanese Navy in what was perhaps the longest naval battle of World War II. This being in the South Pacific and is commonly called the "Battle of Coral Sea." Sometime between May 4 and May 9, 1942 his ship was sunk.

There is a memorial at Manila American Cemetery, Fort Bonifacio, Manila, Philippines of the Missing in Action or Buried at Sea that gives a date of death as May 08, 1943.

Survived by:
Brothers: Edward Barnes of Warsaw; Wallace Barnes, U. S. Navy, New London CT; John Barnes, U. S. Army at Camp Polk, LA; Dell of Batavia; Phillip of Hornell, NY.
Sisters: Arlie Seward of 49 Prospect Ave., Batavia; Bernice Trace of 3 School St. of Batavia; Eunice James of 51 Lyon St. in Batavia.

*The Times, Batavia, NY. – June 3, 1943
**Wyoming County Times* – April 13, 1944
*Wyoming County Veterans Services Office
*National WWII Memorial

Ernest L. Bauer

Sgt., U. S. Army Air Forces

Ernest L. Bauer was born October 23, 1920 in Warsaw, NY. Nicknamed "Ernie," he graduated from Warsaw High School in 1938. He enjoyed playing basketball in school. In his profile in *The Blast*, the school yearbook, he was asked what his desired career would be. His answer was Electrical Engineer; what his probable career would be, his answer was farmer; his saying was, "All things come round to him who will but wait."

He worked on the farm with his father and brother LaVergne and was employed for the Table-Talk Bakery in Batavia. He resided in Erie County, NY prior to the war.

Ernest enlisted August 4, 1942 at Buffalo in the Army Air Force 301st T. C. Squadron, 441st Troop Carrier Group, 473rd Air Service Group where he was a aero-plane mechanic.

On December 23, 1945 he was shot and killed in a non-battle related incident in Berlin, Germany by a man in a Russian uniform. Sgt. Bauer and Technician Fourth Grade Stanley C. Cranston of Warren, RI were killed near Belle Alliance Strasse and Bergmann Strasse near Tempelhof Airport. Military police applied first aid to Cranston. They soon discovered Bauer in the gutter, about 30 yards away, with a 38 cal. bullet wound to the forehead.

Military Police found a revolver which had not been fired in Cranston's pocket. Bauer was unarmed. Six empty shells were found nearby.

Sgt. Bauer is buried at Lorraine American Cemetery, Saint Avold (Moselle), France His parents head stone in Warsaw Cemetery says In Memory of Sgt. Ernest L. Bauer.

Survived by:
Parents: John H. and Lucy Bauer of Rte. 20A, Warsaw and 25 Prospect St.
Brother: La Vergne Bauer of Warsaw. Medically discharged from Army.
Sister: Mrs. Clifford Norton, also of Warsaw.
Aunt: Mrs. Loren Morell of 37 Vine St. in Batavia.

Wyoming County Times – October 5, 1944
New York Post – December 27, 1945
Perry Record – December 27, 1945
Western New Yorker – December 27, 1945; January 17, 1946
* *The Blast*, Warsaw High School Year Book, 1938
*National WWII Memorial website

William H. Browne

Sgt., U. S. Army

William H. Browne enlisted in the Army on December 3, 1942 out of Buffalo, NY. He is noted as being employed as a retail manager. He reported to Fort Niagara on December 9th.

William was stationed at Fort Knox, Kentucky where he received a detailed knowledge of engines, power trains, suspension systems and other elements of the complex tank mechanism for keeping the Army's tanks in fighting trim. This included both Diesels and gasoline engines.

On July 13, 1944, he married Jane M. Austin at St. Michaels Rectory in Warsaw.

During the war he served as a Sergeant, 48th Tank Battalion in the 14th Armored Division.

He was sent overseas in October 1944 to the European Theater where in January 11, 1945 in France he was reported missing and killed in action. He is buried in Lorraine American Cemetery and Memorial, Saint Avold (Moselle), France Section E Row 43 Grave 29.

Survived by:
Wife: Jane (Austin) Browne of Warsaw.
Daughter: Jennifer ~ infant
Mother: Mrs. William H. Browne of Buffalo. (Parents were former residents at 241 N. Main St. in Warsaw.)
Sisters: Doris M. Browne of Buffalo, NY; Lt. Regina Browne U. S. Army, Camp Upton, Long Island, NY.

**Wyoming County Times* – September 2, 1943; September 12, 1943; May 10, 1945; July 27, 1944
**Rochester Times-Union* – May 15, 1945
*National WWII Memorial website

Alexander Dubovy

Tech 5th Grade U. S. Army

Alexander Dubovy was born on February 25, 1915 in Montreal, Quebec, Canada. He entered the service on April 2, 1942 and trained at Pine Camp and Camp Bowie, Texas. He participated in maneuvers in Tennessee and Desert Training in California with the 94th Armored Field Artillery Battalion, 4th Armored Division Battery B, and arose to Rank Technician 5th Grade.

On December 29, 1943 he was sent to England for six months and landed at

Normandy, France July 11, 1944. He was killed in action on September 1, 1944 at Commercy, France.

His body arrived on October 22nd at Weeks Funeral Home in Warsaw under military escort. Services were conducted by a Russian Greek Orthodox priest from Buffalo and Wyoming County Veterans, with full military rites. Alexander was buried in Warsaw Cemetery.

Survived by:
Parents: Kasen and Mary Dubovy of 108 Linwood Ave. in Warsaw.
Brothers: Michael and Walter, both of Warsaw.
Sisters: Miss Mary Dubovy and Mrs. Anne Herrmann both of Warsaw; Mrs. Olga McBurney of LeRoy, NY; Mrs. Helen Weber of Pavilion, NY.

Wyoming County Times – November 26, 1942; October 21, 1948
*Wyoming County Veterans Services Office
*Application for Military Headstone or Marker

Eddy Vernon Fenner

Pvt., U. S. Army

Eddy Vernon Fenner was born May 16, 1925 in Warsaw. In the *Blast* yearbook, graduation class of 1943, Eddy described his ambition as Veterinarian. A quote from him was, "An angel clad in white is she, who stole this very heart from me." He was going to Cornell University to study veterinary medicine; however, he respected his country and his call to duty.

He entered the service on April 26, 1944 and was sent overseas in October of 1944 where he joined the 3rd Army under General George Patton, fighting the Germans in France. He served with 317th Infantry Regiment, 80th Infantry Division.

One month later on November 28, 1944 in Lorraine, France he was killed in action at the age of 19. He is buried in Lorraine American Cemetery, Saint Avold, (Moselle) France in Plot K, Row 11, Grave 6. He was posthumously awarded the Purple Heart.

Survived by:
Parents: Vernon P. and Lila (Madison) Fenner of Oatka Rd. in Warsaw.
Sisters: Miss Nora Jane Fenner Lowden, at home; Mrs. Eleanor Whipple of Akron, Ohio.

*Western New Yorker – January 4, 1945
*Batavia Daily News – December 11, 1999
*The Blast, Warsaw High School yearbook, 1943.
*Wyoming County Veterans Services Office
*National WWII Memorial website

Harry W. Gumaer Jr.

2nd Lt., U. S. Army Air Forces

Harry W. Gumaer Jr. was born on July 28, 1923 in Buffalo, NY. His family moved to Warsaw in the 1930s where he graduated from Warsaw High School in 1940. In his high school years he was involved in the Library Club, band, Photo Club, French Club and the senior play. A quote from his yearbook reads, "Is it a good brain that causes a big head?" He was an honor student and received the Rensselaer Polytechnic Institute Medal and was offered a New York state scholarship. He declined the scholarship to enter the University of Michigan for a course in Aeronautical Engineering for a short time before enlisting in the Army in July 1942. He had completed two years of college and had plans to finish his courses after the war.

His basic training was at Maxwell Field, Alabama. He trained in the states for two years receiving his wings and commission as a 2nd Lt. in the Air Force as a pilot at Brooks Field, San Antonio, Texas. He was sent overseas in February 1944 being based in Italy serving with the U.S. Army Air Forces 515th Bomber Squadron, 376th Bomber Group as a pilot of a twin engine bomber.

Associated Press had reported that on the 22nd of February, bombers in Italy attacked two Messerschmitt plane plants at Regensburg and hit objectives in Italy with a loss of 15 planes. His mother had only received a letter the day before on his arrival in Italy. She received word on March 23, 1944 that her son was reported missing in action when his plane failed to return after the raid. In a letter to the Veteran's office on May 15th , in regards to his war bonds not arriving since his going missing she writes, "Have not received any further word, however, I'm sure he is safe and that I will hear one of these days." She would later learn that his was one of the planes shot down and all on board were killed. 2nd Lt. Gumaer is buried in the Lorraine American Cemetery and Memorial, Saint Avold (Moselle), in France: Plot J, Row 22, Grave 3. He was posthumously awarded the Purple Heart.

Survived by:
Mother: Mrs. Gladys R. Gumaer (and the late Harry W. Gumaer, Sr.) 208 N. Main St. in Warsaw`.
Sister: Miss Sally Gumaer, also of Warsaw.

**Western New Yorker* – June 18, 1942
**Wyoming County Times* – March 23, 1944
* *The Blast*, Warsaw High School yearbook, 1940
*Wyoming County Veterans Services Office
*National WWII Memorial website

Hobby Haven and the *Warsaw Flying Club*

William N. Knight

Sgt., U. S. Army

William Noble Knight was born on October 1, 1921 in Warsaw. He attended Warsaw High School into his sophomore year at which time, at age 16, he entered the workforce. He attended the Presbyterian Church and Sunday school.

On February 16, 1940 he enlisted in the U. S. Army after basic training he was assigned to an anti-aircraft battery on the island of Corregidor at the entrance to Manila Bay. He was with the 60th Coast Artillery Regiment Battery H.

He quickly rose to the rank of Corporal and was put in charge of his anti-aircraft battery consisting of ten men. On December 10, 1941, three days after the Japanese attacked Pearl Harbor and war began for the United States, the anti-aircraft batteries on Corregidor shot down twelve out of fifteen Japanese bombers that attacked them.

In May 1942 the Corregidor forces surrendered to the Japanese. For the next three years Corporal Knight's life as a Japanese prisoner of war was one of brutal treatment. For about eighteen months he was at Camp Cabanatuan north of Manila. Later he was moved to the Japanese home islands to Fukuoka Camp 17 and forced into slave labor in a nearby coal mine. On May 15, 1945 he was accused of taking extra buns by Lt. Cmdr. Little who supervised the mess hall. Knight was tied to a post and beaten by his Japanese guards, deprived of food and water, and died four days later.

At the war time trial, which was held in secrecy in June of 1947, Capt. Isao Fukuhara the Commandant of the Omuta, Fukuoka Prison and another Japanese commander were found guilty of the death of William N. Knight and two other soldiers. They was sentenced to death and executed. Edward N. Little was acquitted of all charges of "maltreatment" of fellow Americans.

At the time, local Veterans from Wyoming County Veterans Association, the Walter Klein Post and the American Legions voiced their concerns and condemned the secret court martial trials that were held and the outcome of Edward Little being acquitted of all his charges.

Sgt. Knight is buried in Manila American Cemetery in Fort Bonifacio, Manila, Philippines, Plot B, Row 5, grave 12. His name has been placed "In Memory of our Son" on his parent's headstone in the Warsaw Cemetery.

Survived by:
Parents: Harold and Alice Knight of Warsaw.
Sisters: Patricia Knight, at home; Sgt. Gloria Knight U. S. Army.

Wyoming County Times – June 12, 1947; October 25, 1945; December 11, 1947; February 7, 1946; February 15, 1940
The Daily News, Batavia, NY. June 14, 1947

Buffalo Courier Express – June 18, 1947
Western New Yorker – June 19, 1947; May 30, 1946; October 25, 1945
Buffalo Evening News – December 18, 1947
*Wyoming County Veterans Services Office
*National WWII Memorial

Note to Reader: In 2010, the author wrote a story entitled *Freedom Is Not Free*, a true story of Sgt. Knight's very tragic five year service to his country in the U. S. Army, most of which was spent as a Japanese prisoner of war. A copy of this story is on file at the Wyoming County Historian's Office and the Warsaw Public Library.

Maurice T. Lester

Store Keeper 2nd Class,
U. S. Navy

Maurice T. Lester was born February 16, 1912 in Warsaw. He attended and graduated from Warsaw High School in 1930. While in school he participated in the senior play and went on the Washington Trip. A quote in his senior year was, "Last year I was a young lad." He was a member of the Warsaw Masonic Lodge.

He enlisted in the Navy at Buffalo, NY on November 11, 1942 and was a storekeeper and ship's cook.

Maurice died October 24, 1944 at Bethesda Naval Hospital in Bethesda, MD, at the age of 32, following an operation. His funeral service was held at Week's Funeral Home followed by a Masonic Ceremony during his burial at Warsaw Cemetery.

Survived by:
Parents: Arthur H. and Frances (Tice) Lester

Rochester Times-Union – October 25, 1944
Wyoming County Times – October 26, 1944
Buffalo Courier Express – October 28, 1944
The Blast, Warsaw High School yearbook, 1930

Wilson F. Marzolf

Pvt. 1st Class, U.S. Army

Wilson F. Marzolf was one of triplets, born on February 24, 1913 in Strykersville, NY to Bernard and Luella Glaser Marzolf. Wilson was a member of the St. Michael's Church and Knights of Columbus. He graduated from Warsaw High School. His motto alongside his photo was, "What this country needs is a good five cent dime." He was actively involved in baseball and basketball serving as manager as well as speedball, softball and track. He was on the student council and a member of the Glee Club. Wilson was known to his friends as "Marzie."

He attended St. Bonaventure College and Manlius Academy USROTC with the ambition of becoming an army officer. He married Helen N. Nugent of Warsaw on November 11, 1936. They owned the Farmer's Lunch on Frank St. in Warsaw. In March of 1937, along with Joseph Nugent, he purchased the Glasier Garage on Genesee St. to convert into a restaurant.

Wilson enlisted into the service from Buffalo on November 9, 1943. He came home from Camp Belding, FL on leave in early June of 1944 to stay with his wife at her parents in Warsaw. After his furlough he reported to Fort George Mead, MD.

Later that same month he was sent overseas and served with the 142nd Infantry, 36 Infantry Division. On January 29, 1945 he was killed in action near Strasbourg, France. His remains were returned home in September of 1948. Burial was in St. Nicholas Cemetery in North Java, NY.

Survived by:
Wife: Helen (Nugent) Marzolf who resided with her parents Mr. and Mrs. John Nugent of 16 Palmer St. Warsaw, NY. (Helen remarries _____ Wagonblass.)
Parents: Luella (Glazier) Marzolf (and the late Bernard A. Marzolf).
Triplet brother: Bernard Marzolf of East Aurora, NY.
Triplet sister: Mrs. Florence Dipenza of Jamestown, NY.
Sister: Mrs. Edward J. George of North Java, NY.

Attica News –February 7, 1935; November 26, 1936; June 8, 1944
Perry Record – February 15, 1944
Wyoming County Times – March 18, 1937; October 27, 1938; June 15, 1944; February 15, 1945; September 9, 1948
*Wyoming County Veterans Services Office

Melvin Otto Miller

Pvt. 1ˢᵗ Class, U. S. Army

Melvin Otto Miller was born in Webster, NY on September 5, 1924. When he was a young boy he came to Warsaw to live. He was known as "Skeet" by his Warsaw High School classmates of which he graduated in 1942. In his high school years he was an all-around sportsman participating in tennis, basketball, football, baseball, and volleyball. He was the president of the junior class, Hi-Y Club, on *The Blast* year book staff and secretary and treasurer of the senior class. A quote from the senior year was "World, here I come—tall, tan and terrific!"

He entered the service on April 6, 1943. He trained in Missouri, Mississippi and at Fort Benning, Georgia before going overseas as a member of the 168th Infantry Regiment, 34th Division in Italy. On April 17, 1945, at age 21, he was killed in action in the Italian Campaign fighting the Germans. He is buried at Florence American Cemetery and

Memorial in Via Cassia, Italy in Plot D, Row 4, Grave 27. He was awarded the Purple Heart posthumously.

Survived by:
Parents: Otto W. and Edith E. Larson Miller of 55 Jackson St., Warsaw.
Brother: Pfc. Merton E. Miller U. S. Army, Fort Benning, Georgia.

Western New Yorker - May 3, 1945
The Blast, Warsaw High School yearbook, 1942
*National WWII memorial

John Francis Schwab

Pvt. 1st Class, U. S. Army

John Francis Schwab was born in Sheldon, NY on May 27, 1923. In 1936 his family moved to 29 Summit Avenue in Warsaw where he lived until he entered the service. He was a 1941 graduate of Warsaw High School. In school he participated in track, Dramatic Club, senior play, band, and orchestra. He was employed for a time at the Buffalo Arms Corp. in Buffalo before entering the military.

He was inducted into the service on October 6, 1943 at Camp Upton, NY. Pvt. Schwab went overseas in March of 1944 to North Africa. He fought in the Italian Campaign and later participated in the invasion of France.

On September 27, 1944 he was reported missing in action and later as killed in action in France. His remains were brought back to his home on Summit Avenue on May 19, 1948 by military escort. A Guard of Honor was maintained at the house until the military service was held that Monday on May 24th for the family, followed by a mass service at St. Michael's Catholic Church. Burial was in St. Michael's Cemetery.

Survived by:
Parents: Augustus and Anna R. (Crahan) Schwab of Warsaw.
Brothers: Robert J., Francis J., Raymond A., and Bernard T. Schwab
Sisters: Cecelia R., Margaret M., Teresa L., Marie G., Eleanor F., Irene A., Rosemarie, and Joan E. Schwab

*Wyoming Reporter – May 27, 1948; May 20, 1948
*Western New Yorker – November 2, 1944
*Rochester Times Union – November 2, 1944
*The Blast, Warsaw High School yearbook, 1941
**Wyoming County Veterans Services Office

James Walter Scott

Cpl., U. S. Army

James Walter Scott was born in Warsaw on November 15, 1919. He enlisted on February 2, 1942 in Buffalo, NY. He was married to Helen Gardner on October 18, 1942.

He was a Corporal of Co. C. 46th Armored Infantry Battalion, 5 Armored Division. He was sent overseas in February 1944 where he saw action in France and Germany.

The 46th Infantry Regiment was assigned to the 5th Armored Division, landing at Normandy in 1944. The 46th Infantry led the 5th Armored Division in five campaigns earning the nickname "Victory's Spear Point."

On December 2, 1944 he was killed in action in one of the largest American offenses called the Battle of the Hurtgen Forest during the second phase, code named *Operation Queen*, in Germany. He has been in the army almost three years and overseas nearly a year when his death occurred. His wife received the Purple Heart awarded to her husband, posthumously. Cpl. Scott is buried in Glenwood Cemetery in Perry.

Survived by:
Wife: Helen Gardner Scott of 115 Linwood Ave. in Warsaw. (Later remarried _____ Gartley.)
Step-Daughter: Sandra Joan
Parents: Walter H. and Lulu E. Scott of Middle Reservation Rd. in Castile.
Brothers: Lynn, Floyd and Zane Scott of Warsaw; Sgt. Gordon Scott, U. S. Army overseas.
Other siblings: Orma, Florice, and Ernest who predeceased James.

Wyoming County Times – January 4, 1945
Western New Yorker – February 1, 1945
*Wyoming County Veterans Services Office

Duane W. Stevens

2nd Lt., U. S. Army Air Forces

DUANE STEVENS

Senior Play, 4; Former student of Fryeburg Academy, Maine.

Duane W. Stevens was born December 12, 1923 in Mercer, Maine. His family had moved to Warsaw in 1940 and lived at 51 Park Street. Before coming to Warsaw, he was a former student of Fryeburg Academy in Maine. He was a 1941 graduate of Warsaw High School participating in the senior play and was a member of the Congregational Church in Warsaw.

He had enlisted in December 1942 and had been commissioned a 2nd Lt. on June 26, 1944 while serving at Luke Field, Phoenix, AZ.

As a Cadet Pilot he was scheduled to be an instructor and was taking special training for that branch of service. While he and a student pilot were flying a plane six miles from Sequin, Texas on August 2, 1944 it crashed killing them both. He had only one more week of training to complete his advanced training.

His body was returned home from Randolph Field, Texas under military escort. His service was held at the United Church in Warsaw with grave side service conducted by the Walter Klein Post. Lt. Stevens was buried in the Warsaw Cemetery.

Survived by:
Parents: Raymond H. and Inez (Hayden) Stevens
Brothers: Thomas A., Clair W., Roland, and Raymond H. Stevens Jr. (who was soon to go into the service) all of Warsaw; Pvt. James H. Stevens U.S. Army, Geiger Field, WA; Cpl. Duncan A. Stevens U. S. Air Force, Plant Park, Tampa, FL.
Sisters: Ruth O. Stevens of Warsaw; Eva Stevens, student at Cortland University; Lucille Stevens, Nurse Cadet at Belleview Hospital in NYC.
Grandmother: Mrs. Fannie A. Stevens of Houston, TX.

Wyoming County Times – August 10, 1944
The Blast, Warsaw High School yearbook, 1941

David Dodge Wallace

2nd Lt., U. S. Army Air Forces

David D. Wallace was born in Caneadea, NY on January 7, 1919. He was a 1936 graduate of Warsaw High School. A quote from a senior yearbook was, "A gentleman is often seen, but seldom heard to laugh." He was involved in Interclass Basketball in his last year of attendance. He was a member of the National Guard prior to the war.

He enlisted in the Army Air Corps on August 23, 1941 at Camp Stewart, Hinesville, GA. In the fall of that year, he transferred to the Air Corp at Keesler Field, Mississippi. In December 1942 he started pre-flight training at Maxwell Field, AL, graduating from Stuttgart, Army Air Field, AK, in August of 1943. He finished his training at March Field in California before being sent overseas in January 1944.

On March 6, 1944 while serving as co-pilot of a B-24 Liberator bomber with the 733rd Bomber Squadron, 453rd Bomber Group, his plane was severely damaged by flak over their target and again near the European mainland on their return from a mission over Genshagen,

Germany. In attempting to return the plane to its 8th Air Force base in England, it was apparent the plane could not reach land. The entire crew parachuted out over the North Sea near Yarmouth, England. Five members survived and five members including David D. Wallace perished. His body was never recovered.

He is memorialized in the Cambridge American Cemetery on the Tablets of the Missing in Cambridgeshire, England. He was posthumously awarded the Purple Heart with one Oak Leaf Cluster.

Survived by:
Father: William Wallace of W. Buffalo St. in Warsaw.
Brothers: Lyle Wallace of Rochester, NY; Neal Wallace of LeRoy, NY.
Sister: Mrs. Flora Washburn of Fillmore, NY.

The Leroy Gazette News – July 6, 1944
Wyoming County Times – July 6, 1944
The Blast, Warsaw High School yearbook, 1936
*National World War II Memorial
*Wyoming County Veterans Services Office

Walter Jerome Wilcox Jr.

Pvt., U. S. Army

Walter Jerome Wilcox Jr. was born in Warsaw on May 21, 1921. He graduated from Warsaw High School in 1940. A quote from his senior yearbook was "We fell out, my gal and I, We fell out, I know not why."

He enlisted in the National Guard of New York on December 4, 1940 and was inducted into the military service on February 10, 1941 at Rochester, NY. He joined the 209th Coast Artillery which left for Camp Stewart, GA. He was as a member of an anti-aircraft unit.

While out on a seven hour pass in a civilian car near Ways Station, GA, Private Wilcox was killed instantly and the soldier with him, Jack O. Vickers of Rochester, was seriously injured when they had a sideswipe with a truck and trailer between Savannah and Pinesville on December 13, 1941. He was 20-years-old. His remains were escorted home by Pfc. Stewart Perkins of Warsaw as the Guard of Honor. His service was held at the Baptist Church on the 19th of December. He was buried in Warsaw Cemetery.

Survived by:
Parents: Walter J. and Clara (Morgan) Herman Wilcox of Wethersfield Rd. (later of 30 Butternut) in Warsaw.
Half-brother: Leslie Morgan, also of Warsaw.

Buffalo Courier Express – December 15, 1941
Western New Yorker - December 18, 1941
The Blast, Warsaw High School yearbook, 1940
*Wyoming County Veterans Services Office

James L. Woodley

1st in US Navy, 2nd as a Pvt., U. S. Army

James L. Woodley was born in Warsaw on July 15, 1928. He was a member of the Methodist Church. He attended Warsaw High School but left at age 15 in his sophomore year to join the service. James gave his age as 17 and joined the Navy on December 9, 1943. Several months in he was stricken with appendicitis. His parents were contacted by the navel authorities when his true age was revealed. The Navy had no choice but to discharge him. After recovering at home from surgery, he joined the Army's amphibious division, harbor craft.

On Christmas Day, 1944 on Black Mesa Mountain, 30 miles east of Blythe, California, an Army transport plane crashed. Seventeen servicemen were killed— thirteen passengers and a crew of four. The plane was a C-47 based out of the Malden, Missouri Air Transport Command Field. It cleared Tucson, Arizona on Christmas morning on route to Palm Springs, California. It crashed at Quartzite, AZ. Difficulties encountered in getting to the wreckage and removing the victims resulted in a delay in identifying those killed in the crash; and it was not until January 6, 1945 that James could be identified. His burial was on January 11, 1945 at Warsaw Cemetery.

Survived by:
Parents: Claude B. and Bonnie Ethel (Liggett) Woodley of Warsaw.
Brothers: Paul E. Woodley of Warsaw (a good friend of the author); Lt. Claude Woodley, U. S. Air Force in France.
Sisters: Loraine Woodley of Warsaw; Mrs. Claude Bush of Dale.
Grandparents: Mr. and Mrs. Walter Woodley of Warsaw; Mrs. Henry Liggett of Lewisburg, TN.

Rochester Times Union – January 9, 1945
Wyoming County Times – January 11, 1945
*Another newspaper article untitled and undated
*Wyoming County Veterans Services Office

Gordon Keith Wright

1st Lt., U. S. Army

Gordon Keith Wright was born in Olean, NY on September 20, 1917. At age five, he moved with his family to Warsaw where he graduated from Warsaw High School in 1935. While in school he participated in basketball, football, track, Hi-Y, Treasurer of Class, and "Dollars to Doughnuts." A quote from his senior year was, "A little nonsense now and then is relished by the wisest men." He was also a member of the Methodist Church. He took a post graduate course before entering Indiana University College where he took an administrative course in Commercial Law. He entered the auditing department of the General Electric Co. in Schenectady, NY.

He joined the Army in February of 1943 and was sent overseas in March of 1945 as a member of the 97th Infantry Division arriving in the

JAMES GILLEN

European Theater in April. He achieved the rank of 1st Lt. at Fort Benning, Georgia.

While engaged in battle, crossing the Sieg River in Siegburg, Germany on April 9, 1945 he was killed in action.

He was posthumously awarded the Silver Star. This award is announced by Major General H. F. Kramer's 97th Infantry Division, only division redeployed from Europe to Japan.

His citation reads, "Awarded for gallantry in action on 9 April, 1945. Lt. Wright, commander of the company headquarters group of a rifle company, led an assault across the Sieg River against a fortified factory area in Siegburg, Germany. He drove rapidly forward with his men against severe enemy opposition.

Later regrouping two badly disorganized rifle platoons. He bravely led the final assault in which he was mortally wounded. Lt. Wright's gallantry aided immeasurably in the successful accomplishment of the company's mission and reflects great credit upon himself and the Armed forces."

At the time of the action described in the citation, the 97th Infantry was participating in the subjugation of the encircled Ruhr Pocket. With Lt. Wright's brave leadership, a fortified castle was captured in Siegburg which had previously succeeded in arresting the forward movement of an entire battalion of 97th Division Infantrymen.

According to a letter dated February 12, 1946 from Army Services Forces, Washington, D.C. it states, "The official Report of Burial discloses that the remains of your son were interred in Plot YY, Row 7, Grave 166 in the United States Military Cemetery, Margraten, Holland, located approximately twelve miles northwest of Aachen, Germany and eight miles southeast of Maastricht, Holland." However, according to the American War Cemetery Margraten and the WWII Memorial, he is in

Plot M, Row 17, Grave 2. There is also a stone in Mount View Cemetery in Olean, NY with his name inscribed along with his parents.

Survived by:
Parents: Seth W. and Phoebe Wright of 43 Center Street in Warsaw.
Brothers: S. W. Wright Jr. of Doylestown, Ohio; Max B. Wright of Buffalo, NY; David J. Wright, Navy Seabees Guam.
Sisters: Mrs. J. P. Flood of Washington, D.C.; Mrs. Kermit Greene of Meadville, PA.

Wyoming County Times – December 31, 1942; April 26, 1945; July 5, 1945
Western New Yorker – April 25, 1946
The Blast, Warsaw High School yearbook, 1935
*Wyoming County Veterans Services Office
*National WWII Memorial

Truck Load of Jacket Floss

A truckload of milkweed pods totaling 2½ tons, all collected by youngsters in the Warsaw area, is shown here ready to be shipped for use in making life jackets for the armed forces. More than 2,100 school children participated in the Wyoming County campaign, collecting 3,145 bushels of the pods, enough to make 1,578 life jackets.

Rochester Times Union— Mon., October 30, 1944.

Image from *The Torch*, Attica High School yearbook, 1944

CHAPTER SEVENTEEN

Wethersfield

The Town of Wethersfield historian reports that no Wethersfield residents lost their lives serving their country during World War II. There is also none listed in the *World War II Honor List of Dead and Missing, State of New York*, (War Dept. 1946)

Iashima. Japanese board C-54 to fly to Manila to talk to General Douglas McArthur. August 19, 1945. *Collection of Author James Gillen. Taken by his friend, George Clair*

Photographs by Nicholas Dovolos from his WWII photo album titled "England 1943 to France 1944 to Home 1945." *Photos courtesy of his son, George Dovolos.*

CHAPTER EIGHTEEN

Attributed to Wyoming

Out of County Soldiers

Through additional research at the Wyoming County Historian's office it was discovered that there were soldiers who were attributed to Wyoming County, via a variety of newspaper or state lists, who were in fact residents elsewhere. To avoid confusion, they are honored here along with credit to their hometowns.

NL – Wartime Newspaper List
SL – *World War II Honor List of Dead and Missing State of New York* (1946)

CAPT. HERSEL R. ADAMS – (SL) The only Hersel Adams we found was from Mineola, TX, but was indeed a Captain with the 141st Infantry 36th Division, Army. He died September 9, 1943. He is buried in Nettuno (Permanent) Cemetery, Italy; Block G, Row 13, Grave 9. He received the Purple Heart and the Distinguished Service Cross.

JAMES W. BAKER – (NL) Pharmacist Mate, First Class; entered the Navy in 1942. He was from Franklinville, NY. He died from Spinal Meningitis on January 4, 1945 and was buried at sea. He was 28-years-old. PMFC Baker is memorialized at the Brittany American Cemetery, St. James (Manche), France.

SGT. ELTON A. DUKELMAN – (SL) We found no record whatsoever. We believe it could be a typo of Alton E. Dukelow.

PVT. FRANK E. GOODFELLOW – (NL) Frank was from Marilla, Erie County, NY. He entered the service in Buffalo on April 22, 1943. Pvt. Goodfellow was with the US Army, 30th Infantry Regiment, 3rd Infantry Division. He was killed on the Italian Front on January 25, 1944. He was 18-years-old. His mother Sadie, at that time lived on East Blood Road with a Cowlesville mailing address. She worked at Curtis-Wright in Buffalo. She was back to work the next day saying, "Maybe I can keep some other boys from being killed." Pvt. Goodfellow is buried in the Sicily-Rome American Cemetery in Nettuno, Italy in Plot I, Row 7, Grave 34. He received the Purple Heart, posthumously.

PFC ARLAND CLAIR KELLEY – (NL) He was born in Dalton in Livingston County on July 7, 1921 and later a resident of Cayuga County. He was with the US Army, Company E, 424th Infantry, 106th Infantry Division. PFC Kelley was killed in action in Belgium on February 14, 1945. He is buried in Woodlawn National Cemetery in Chemung County, NY.

TECH SGT. JOHN J. KREYER JR. – (SL) Army Air Corps. He was born in 1923. He was a resident of Suffolk County, NY. He enlisted in New York City on October 27, 1942. He is buried in the Long Island National Cemetery.

STAFF SGT. CARLTON H. LAPP – (NL) A resident of Darien in Genesee County. He was killed on January 31, 1943 on Leyte in the Philippines. He was brought home to be buried in September of 1948 in the Darien Center Cemetery.

2ND LT. CHARLES P. LOGEL JR. – (NL) He appears in the Strykersville column in newspapers, but he was from East Aurora. He was the son of Alice and Carl P. Logel. His mother, later remarried to Harry Handel and lived at 494 Oakwood Avenue. According to his enlistment record he was born in Ohio. He enlisted as a private in the Air Corp on August 31, 1942. His civil occupation stated he was skilled in building of aircraft. He served with the 87th Fighter Squadron, 79th Fighter Group, US Army Air Force. The Strykersville column of March 16, 1944 said he "figured in an invader mission north of Rome, Friday, when he scored a direct bomb hit on buildings used by German gun crews as barracks." He was shot down over Northern Italy on May 24, 1944. He was returned home for burial in 1948 and was laid to rest in Immaculate Conception Church Cemetery in East Aurora.

2ND LT. THOMAS J. MEWHORT JR. – (SL) Thomas was from Richmond, NY; born in 1917. He enlisted in the Army at Fort Jay Governors Island on May 25 1942. He was with 347th Infantry, 87th Division. He died on March 25, 1945. He was buried in Hamm (Permanent Cemetery) Luxembourg; Block A, Row 3, Grave 20. He received the Purple Heart, posthumously.

PVT. JESSE ARTHUR NEWMAN – (NL) United States Marine Corp. Jesse and his wife Ella M. Newman were from Chaffee, NY. He was born on June 29, 1921. He was killed in action in Okinawa on May 21, 1945. He is buried at the Honolulu Memorial in Hawaii in Plot F, Row 1, Grave 25. He received the Purple Heart, posthumously. A memorial service was held on September 23rd that year at the Chaffee Baptist Church where his wife was presented the Gold Star.

2ND LT. MARTIN E. SALWAY JR. – (NL) Martin hailed from Batavia, NY. He was born March 13, 1916 and was a graduate of Batavia High School in 1935, attended college in Toledo for two years, then returned home to operate the Atlantic Service Station at East Main St. and Clinton. His parents lived at 210 W. Main Street. Martin entered the Air Force in January of 1942 shortly after marrying Mary (Shreder) on New Year's Day. He earned his wings in February of 1943. Lt. Salway was a pilot of a Liberator bomber. He was killed on September 15, 1943 during a strike on German occupied Europe. Martin's wife Mary, originally from Attica, went on to teaching at Brewster College in Putnam County.

STAFF SGT. RICHARD L. SICK – (NL) Richard was born in Canaseraga, son of James L. and Myra (Fay) Sick. They lived in Kanona for a time and he attended Haverling High School in Bath. By 1940 his father was living in Castile and Richard is on the 1940 census as a farm hand there. (At the time of his death his mother is not listed as surviving him.) He entered the service in December of 1942 while working in Buffalo at the Curtis-Wright plant and sent overseas in December the following year. He was part of the Army Air Force, 21st Squadron, 91st Air Depot Group. He was killed in a plane crash near France on November 1, 1944. Richard was buried in Plot F, Row 16, Grave 40 of the Henri-Chaeplle American Cemetery in Belgium. He was survived by his wife Emily Jane and an infant son, Donald.

MAJ. HARRY B. STOKES – (NL) Harry was born in India on July 21, 1904. He spent his childhood in London. He came to America at about 20 years of age and attended Oxford. He later studied medicine at the University of Michigan and worked at various hospitals before moving to Omaha. He enlisted in the Army Medical Corp in June of 1942. He was killed in action in North Africa on January 2, 1943. His wife Helen (Crawford) Stokes and their two daughters, Susan and Shelly, were living with her parents at 19 Jefferson Street in Warsaw while her husband was in the service. Maj. Stokes is buried in the North African American Cemetery in Carthage, Tunisia in Plot H, Row 12, Grave 6. A memorial inscription is on his wife's tombstone in Warsaw Cemetery.

PFC. ALTON W. STRASBURG – (NL) Alton was born in 1924, a resident of Niagara County. He enlisted out of Buffalo on March 11, 1943. He was with the 141st Infantry, 36th Division. He was killed on August 14, 1944. He is buried at Rhone, Draguignan, France. Pfc. Strasburg was a recipient of the Purple Heart and Bronze Star.

Acknowledgements

As publishers, we wish to express our appreciation to the family members of our soldiers and our community organizations for answering our call for biographical information and photographs via word of mouth and ads in local papers. Our apologies if we have missed anyone on our list below, and our sincere thanks to all of ySteinou. What started as one man's life long ambition, was completed by a community's respect for those in Wyoming County who made the ultimate sacrifice. Two years of additional research by myself, Cindy Amrhein, and my assistant Sally Smith of the Wyoming County Historians Office, helped to complete Mr. Gillen's dream. Out of 103 men, we are only lacking 15 photographs. Although every attempt has been made for accuracy from the information available, you may still find what you will consider an error. Also, if a soldier had a connection with one of our towns we included him, even if he is not listed among a town's official list of MIA/KIA for WWII.

Cindy Amrhein ~ Wyoming County Historian
Sally Smith ~ Asst. County Historian

100th BG Foundation, www.100thbg.com (Basil Numack photo)
Tara Alexander (Harold Q. Bostian photo)
Sue Andrews, Arcade Historical Society
Attica Library (yearbooks)
Dave and Jean Bassett (Harry Gumaer Jr. photo w/model plane)
Elizabeth Bates (Theodore Hunt & Eugene Youngberg)
Loraine Bell (James L. Woodley photo)
Scott Bavarian (Leon George & Wilson Marzolf info)
Dave Bodine
Loretta Butler, Pike Town Clerk
Kevin Carlson
Bill Clester
Art Crater (Maurice T. Lester photo)
Christine DeGolyer (Willard T. DeGolyer photo)
Orlo Demun (Rodney O. DeMun photo)
George Devolos (WWII photos by his father Nick Devolos)
Owen E. Eddy (Elmer J. Boatfield photo)
Michael J. Eula, Genesee County Historian (Glenn VanValkenburg photo)
Brian Fugle, Attica Historical Society
Doris Ann (Knack) Fyle (Joseph R. Knack info & photos)
Genesee Falls Town Clerk (Leon & Robert Lathrop photos)
Danielle Gell Arnold (James Gell photo)

Ellen Lori George (Leon George photo)
Cynthia Granger
Edith & Ellen Grant, Bennington Historical Society
Lisa Harvey, Wyoming County Veterans Services
Anita Hayes (John Coons & Robert Gracey photos)
Dick Heye (Robert Boatfield & Jack McGee photos)
Dean June, Attica Historical Society
Robin Kruppa, Wyoming County Veterans Services
Laury Lakas, Orangeville Town Historian
Linda Little, Castile Town Historian
Betty Lowe, Covington Historical Society
Mary Mann, Gainesville Town Historian
Jeff Mason, Arcade Historian
Laurie Lounsberry McFadden, Archivist, Alfred University (John Maher info)
McKelton Post 350 American Legion
Jeanne Mest, Sheldon Historical Society
Doug Norton, Middlebury Town Historian
Perry Public Library (yearbooks and bound Perry newspapers)
Perry Vets Club (Several photos of Perry's KIA soldiers)
John Powers (Jack McGee photo)
Jack Rase (Grant G. Stout)
Nina Duboy Reisdorf (Alexander Dubovy photo)
Joanne Ripstein, Attica Town Historian
Carl Rodson (Thomas P. O'Brien photo)
Keith Rowe (Richard A. Rowe photos)
Laurie Saunders (Joseph R. Knack)
Walter Scott (Alton E. Dukelow photo)
Helen Shaw (Robert K. Gracey)
Ann Smith, Eagle History Center
Mike Spellicy (Richard N. Spellicy photo)
Judy Stiles, Genesee County Historian's Office (Glenn VanValkenburg)
Bruce Strathearn
Andy Straub (Eugene N. Straub photo)
Matt Surtel (Michael Surtel photo)
Evelyn Taylor (Robert Boatfield)
Lesa VanSon, Bennington Town Historian
Lorraine Wagner, Eagle Town Historian
Shirley Warren, Covington Town Historian
Warsaw Historical Society
Karen Washburn (Richard N. Spellicy)

Index

102nd Coast Artillery Anti-Aircraft Regiment, 39
112th C.A. Transport Detachment, 39
112th Infantry, 28th Division, 108
121st Cavalry of the New York National Guard, 39
141st Infantry Regiment, 36th Infantry, 35
15th Air Forces Flying Fortress Squardron, 63
174th Infantry, Co. I, 7
17th Airborne Division, 71
180th Coast Artillery, 89
180th Infantry Regiment, 45th Infantry Division, 101
193rd Glider Infantry, 17th Airborne Division, Company C, 46
19th Armored Infantry Battalion 14th Armored Division Reconnaissance Group, 12
1st Division 7th Marines, 29
207th Infantry, 16
209th Coast Artillery, 137
275th Engineers 75th Infantry Division, 43
290th Infantry, Co. B, 36
299th Combat Engineers, 10
301st T. C. Squadron, 441st Troop Carrier Group, 473rd Air Service Group, 124
305th Infantry Regiment, 77th Infantry Division, 121
306th Infantry Division in the 3rd Army, 88

311th Infantry Regiment, 78th Infantry Division, 28
318th Infantry Regiment, 80th Infantry Division, Co. G, 79
319 AAF Bomb Group, 6
31st Infantry, 50
322nd Infantry Regiment, 69
324th Infantry Regiment, 44th Infantry Division, 68
330th Infantry Regiment, 83rd Infantry Division, 66
334th Infantry Regiment, the 84th Infantry Division, 96
335 Infantry 84 Division, 54
345th Bombing Group, 498th Squadron, 27
350th Infantry, 88th Division, 99
350th Infantry, 88th Division, 5th Army, 55
351st Infantry, 88th Division, 62, 109
353rd College Training Detachment, 10
35th Engineer Combat Battalion, Co. C, 37
372nd Bomber Squadron, 307th Bomber Group, 61
387 AAF Fighter Squadron, 114
406th Infantry Regiment, Co. D 102nd Ozark Division of the 9th Army, 41
416th Bomb Squadron, 99th Bomb Group, 103
416th Bomber Squadron, 99th Bomb Group, 87
424th Infantry Regiment 106th Infantry Division, 39

46th Infantry, 5th Armored Division, 134
48th Tank Battalion in the 14th Armored Division, 125
4th Marine Division, 33
515th Bomber Squadron, 376th Bomber Group, 127
53rd Armored Engineer Battalion, 8th Armored Division, 23
592nd Engineer Shore Regiment, 90
5th Army, 100
5th Army, 88th Blue Devils Infantry Division-338th Field Artillery, 106
60th Coast Artillery Regiment Battery H, 128
615 Bomber Squadron, 401st Bomber Group, 18
67th Regiment 2nd Armored Division, 117
733rd Bomber Squadron, 453rd Bomber Group, 136
739th Engineer Heavy Shop Company, 11
782nd Army Air Forces Bomber Squadron, 75
787th Bomber Squadron, 466th Bomber Group, Heavy, 97
794th Military Police Battalion, 98
7th Marines, 1st Marine Division, 120
94th Armored Field Artillery Battalion, 4th Armored Division Battery B, 125
96th Bomber Squadron, 2nd Bomber Group, 13
97th Division of Gen. Patton's Army, 36
97th Infantry Division, 139
9th Air Force, 113

Adams, Hersel R., 145
Africa, 13, 21, 55, 57, 62, 63, 98, 105, 133, 148
Air Corps, 10, 15, 44, 49, 136
Air Force, 6, 13, 18, 26, 39, 47, 49, 56, 60, 61, 63, 64, 74, 75, 81, 87, 97, 103, 105, 113, 123, 127, 135, 136, 139
Allen, Roger Robert, 9
Army, 7, 10, 12, 16, 19, 20, 23, 24, 28, 34, 35, 37, 39, 41, 43, 45, 46, 51, 53, 54, 55, 57, 60, 62, 66, 67, 68, 69, 70, 79, 80, 83, 88, 89, 90, 92, 93, 94, 95, 98, 99, 100, 101, 102, 106, 108, 109, 110, 117, 118, 119, 121, 123, 124, 125, 126, 128, 129, 131, 132, 133, 134, 135, 136, 137, 138, 139, 146
Army Reserve, 24
Atwell, William H., 121
Austria, 74
Baker, James W., 145
Ballard, Jesse C., 53
Banks, George William Jr., 10
Barnes, Frank Kenneth, 122
Bataan, 50
Batangas, Luzon, 11
Battery A, 58th Armored Field Artillery, 1st Army, 57
Battle of the Coral Sea Memorial Park, 22
Battles
  Battle of Bastogne, 71
  Battle of Coral Sea, 17, 21, 123
  Battle of Guam, 121
  Battle of Okinawa, 30
  Battle of Salerno, 20, 101
  Battle of St. Vith, 43
  Battle of the Bulge, 37, 66, 71
  Battle of the Ruhr, 23
  Hurtgen Forest, 134

Bauer, Ernest L., 123
Belgium, 28, 37, 39, 41, 43, 57, 58, 65, 66, 71, 114, 146
Boatfield, Elmer J., 41
Boatfield, Robert J., 49
Bostian, Harold Quincy, 79
Browne, William H., 124
Brunswick, 18
Burgett, Charles R., 87
Campaigns
   Asiatic-Pacific Campaign, 73, 120
   European-African, 7
   Sicilian Campaign, 21
   Solomon's Campaign, 96
   Tunisian Campaign, 21
Campbell, Charles Lowell, 12
Cannon, Charles R., 37
Cemeteries
   American Cemetery and Memorial in Tunisia, 98
   American Cemetery in Fort Bonifacio, 61, 129
   Arcade Rural Cemetery, 7
   Ardennes-American Cemetery, 65
   Cambridge American Cemetery, 137
   Chautauqua Cemetery, 12
   Cowlesville Cemetery, 38
   Elmwood Cemetery, 61, 62, 63, 71
   Florence American Cemetery, 100, 107, 132
   Forest Hill Cemetery, 16, 17
   Fort Hill Cemetery, 25
   Glenwood Cemetery, 90, 93, 94, 95, 102, 104, 134
   Grace Cemetery, 45, 74, 75
   Graceland Cemetery, 47
   Grand View Cemetery, 41
   Henri-Chapelle American Cemetery, 28, 39, 66
   Hillside Cemetery, 88
   Hope Cemetery (Castile), 43
   Lakeside Memorial Park Cemetery, 21
   Linwood Cemetery, 110
   Lorraine American Cemetery, 52, 69, 124, 125, 126, 128
   Luxembourg American Cemetery, 38, 58, 67, 80
   Lyonsburg Cemetery, 56
   Manila American Cemetery, 11, 22, 32, 50, 91, 123, 129
   Manila American Cemetery and Memorial, 11, 91, 119
   Maple Grove Cemetery, 57, 69
   Maple Lawn Cemetery (Bolivar), 46
   Military Cemetery No. 3, 25
   Mount View Cemetery, 7, 141
   National Cemetery at Saint Avold, 12
   National Memorial Cemetery of the Pacific, 8, 27, 53
   Netherlands American Cemetery, 18, 96
   Normandy American Cemetery, 118
   Oakwood Cemetery, 48
   Pike Cemetery, 112, 114, 115
   Pine Grove Cemetery (Fillmore), 58
   Pleasant Valley Cemetery, 89
   Pleasant View Cemetery, 119
   Rosendale Plains Cemetery, 23
   Sicily-Rome American Cemetery, 14, 35, 42, 99, 101
   St. Joseph's Cemetery, 110
   St. Laurent (Permanent Cemetery), 83

St. Mary's Cemetery, 60
St. Mary's Cemetery (Pavilion), 52
St. Michael's Cemetery, 120, 133
St. Nicholas Cemetery, 131
St. Peter and Paul Cemetery, 5
St. Stanislaus Cemetery, 97, 108
St. Vincent's Cemetery, 20, 26, 30, 33, 36
US Military Cemetery at Bensheim, 68
US Military Cemetery, Margraten, Holland, 140
Warsaw Cemetery, 124, 126, 129, 130, 136, 138, 139
Wesseloh Cemetery, 65
Wethersfield Cemetery, 54
Woodlawn National Cemetery, 70
Wyoming Cemetery, 80, 82
Zachary Taylor National Cemetery, 106
Co. B, 22nd Reg., 4th Division, 3rd Army, 94
Co. C. 46th Armored Infantry Battalion, 5 Armored Division, 134
Co. G 28th Infantry 8th Division, 95
Co. I 3rd Branch, 7th Regiment, Fleet Marine Force, 112
Co. M, 3rd Battalion, 157th Infantry Regiment, 45th Infantry Division, 7th, 51
Coast Guard, 5, 99
Cocoanut Grove Fire, 5
Concentration Camps
  Camp Cabanatuan, 129
  Camp Dachau, 51
  Fukuoka Camp 17, 129
Conway, James F., 13
Coons, John A., 15

Courtney, Edward James, 59
Czechoslovakia, 36
Czerminski, Kazimier Jozef, 42
Czerwinski, Casimer Joseph, 42
Davis, Kermit Adolph, 43
DeGolyer, Willard T., 44
DeMun, Rodney Orlo, 88
Dortmund, Germany, 113, 114
Dovolos, George, 77
Dovolos, Nicholas, 77, 85, 144
Dubovy, Alexander, 125
Dukar, 98
Dukelman, Elton A., 145
Dukelow, Alton E., 89
Dumbleton, Robert Chasey, 60
Eichenberger, Richard K., 16
Emery, Leonard E., 90
Engineers Corps, 56
Ernst, George Edward, 17
Fenner, Eddy Vernon, 126
Field, William S., 80
Fix, Norman J., 18
Formosa, 27, 114
France, 15, 21, 36, 37, 41, 47, 51, 52, 57, 62, 69, 71, 74, 80, 83, 85, 91, 95, 103, 108, 117, 118, 124, 125, 126, 128, 131, 133, 134, 139, 144, 145, 148
  Baerenthal, 12, 13
  Dunkirk, 91
  Grand Failly, 71
  Imbsheim, 13
  Metz, 12
  Mouterhouse, 13
  Riedheim, 13
Gell, James, 62
Genshagen, Germany, 137
George, Bertrand C., 19
George, Leon W., 117
Germany, 28, 36, 37, 48, 51, 54, 67, 68, 74, 94, 95, 102, 103, 134

Aachen, 140
Anrochte, 18, 23
Berlin, 18, 124
Brakel, 113
Dusseldorf, 36
Halberstadt, 18
Luxembourg, 67, 80
Munich, 51
Oschersleben, 18
Remagen, 37
Reutti, 52
Rhine, 41
Ruhr, 23, 36, 140
Zeven, 65
Glor, Kenneth J., 20
Goodfellow, Frank E., 146
Gracey, Robert Kennedy, 21
Guadalcanal, 29, 31, 73, 96, 102, 112
Gumaer, Harry W. Jr, 127
Hall, Edward Raymond, 92
Hess, Robert J., 54
Hewitt, Ward Samuel, 93
Hickey, George M., 45
Holmes, John W., 46
Honolulu Memorial, 29
Honolulu, Hawaii, 8, 27, 53
Hungary, 74
Hunt, Theodore William, 111
Husted, Paul Clayton, 63
Invasions
   Anzio Beach Invasion, 114
   Casa Blanca Invasion, 114
   Invasion of Cape Gloucester, 112
   Italian Invasion, 57
   Okinawa, 24
Island of Leyte, 82
Island of Luzon, 50
Italy, 6, 14, 20, 28, 35, 51, 55, 62, 63, 74, 75, 98, 99, 100, 101, 102, 103, 106, 107, 109, 110, 114, 127, 128, 132, 145, 146, 147
Florence, 100
Salerno, 20
Iwo Jima, 33
Jackson, Stephen S., 23
Japan, 114, 118, 140, 159
Judd, William Harvey, 94
Kader, Warren George, 55
Kelly, Arland C., 146
Kendari, 82
Knack, Joseph Roger, 95
Knight, William Noble, 128
Kolacinski, Raymond, 96
Kosciolek, Alfred S., 97
Kreyer, John J.Jr., 146
Kuppinger, Harold R., 24
Laird, Richard Francis, 118
Lapp, Carlton H., 146
Lathrop, Leon E., 73
Lathrop, Robert S., 74
Lauer, Donald William Redden, 5
Lester, Maurice T., 130
Lippold, Francis Bernard, 25
Logel, Charles P. Jr., 146
MacArthur, General, 119
Maher, John Edward, 120
Manila, 11, 22, 32, 50, 61, 91, 119, 123, 128, 129, 143
Marianas Islands, 90
Marine Corps, 10, 29, 33, 59, 73, 96, 111, 120
Marino, Bennie P., 98
Marzolf, Wilson F., 131
Mayhew, Robert E., 99
McGee, Jack, 51
Mewhort, Thomas J., 147
Migliore, Horatio, 100
Miller, Melvin Otto, 132
Mulner, Martin H., 26
Munchen-Gladbach, 41

Myers, Donald E., 28
Myitkyina, Burma, 53
National Guard, 35, 39, 103, 136, 137
Navy, 8, 9, 17, 21, 25, 29, 30, 31, 42, 43, 67, 94, 97, 101, 109, 114, 115, 118, 122, 123, 130, 138, 141, 159
Newman, Jesse A., 147
Normandy, 57, 83, 126, 134
Numack, Basil, 64
O'Brien, Thomas Patrick, 66
Okinawa, 17, 25, 114
Pacific Ocean, 61
Parker, Thomas Arthur Jr, 102
Patton, General, 57
Pearl Harbor, 11, 31, 102, 111, 129, 159
Peleliu Island, 10
Peleliu Islands, 73, 120
Phelan, John F., 29
Philippine Islands, 11, 31, 91
Philippines, 11, 22, 32, 50, 61, 70, 90, 91, 102, 114, 119, 123, 129
Planes
    B-17, 14, 63
    B-17 Flying Fortress, 14
    B-17F, 87, 88
    B-17G, 18
    B-24, 74, 97, 136
    B-24 Liberator Bomber, 74
    B-25 bomber, 27
    B-26 bomber, 6
    B-29, 47, 48
    C-47, 139
    Flying Fortress, 18, 57, 63, 65, 87, 103
    Liberator, 18
    P-38, 82
Prentice, Donald Morrow, 103
Prisoner of War, 21, 47, 50, 57, 129, 130
Redden Lauer, Donald William, 5
Reding, Bernard Otto, 29
Rhine River, 37
Rice, Evan Hayes, 6
Rider, Lawrence E., 105
Rissinger, LaVerne Paul, 56
Roberts, Floyd K., 57
Rowe, Richard A., 81
Royal Canadian Army, 91
Rumania, 75
Russell Islands, 102
Salway, Martin E. Jr., 147
Schadt, John A., 83
Schell, Henry P., 67
Schwab, John Francis, 133
Scott, James Walter, 134
Shearing, Walter W., 68
Ships
    Neosho, 21, 22
    USS Bunker Hill, 29
    USS Gansvoort, 17
    USS Hornet, 118
    USS Juneau, 31, 32
    USS Lindsey, 17
    USS Maddox, 42
    USS Marshall, 20
    USS Nicholson, 114
    USS Princeton, 118
    USS Sims, 17, 122
    USS Wyoming, 67
Sicily, 6, 7, 14, 21, 35, 42, 62, 77, 99, 101, 103, 105, 114, 146
Sick, Richard L., 147
Siegburg, Germany, 140
Smith, John H., 69
Snyder, William A., 7
Solomon Islands, 32, 102

South Pacific, 8, 61, 73, 81, 90, 91, 96, 97, 102, 112, 114, 118, 120, 121, 123
Spellicy, Richard N., 106
Spencer, Donald Houghton, 30
Spring, Merrill T., 47
Stevens, Duane W., 135
Stokes, Harry B., 148
Stout, Grant Gates, 113
Strasburg, Alton W., 148
Straub, Eugene Neter, 31
Submarines
    SS-209, 31
    USS Grayling, 31
Summers, Robert H., 39
Surtel, Michael, 108
Switzerland, 87, 88, 103, 104
Theaters
    European Theater, 36, 37, 67, 82, 95, 113, 117, 125, 140
    Mediterranean Theater, 99
    Pacific Theater, 10, 21, 24, 27, 29, 30, 33, 75
Tortorice, Anthony J. Jr., 109
Trace, Herbert C., 110
Van Valkenburg, Glenn Ellsworth, 8
Vella LaVella, 102
Wagner, Theodore Ernest, 70
Wallace, David D., 136
Walsh, Maurice Bernard, 33
War Memorial Chapel, 13
Whaley, Frank R., 34
Wilcox, Walter Jerome Jr, 137
Woodley, James L., 138
Wright, Gordon Keith, 139
Youngberg, Eugene Robert, 114
Yugoslavia, 75
Zahler, Artell Francis, 35

ABOUT THE AUTHOR

JAMES E. GILLEN
WWII Veteran

James Gillen is a life-long resident of Warsaw, NY. Born in 1927, he attended Warsaw High School and graduated in 1944. That year he enlisted in the U.S Navy, serving for two years as an Aviation Ordnanceman. He attended the U.S Navy Technical Training Station at Norman, OK. Gillen served as an instructor at Florida's Jacksonville Naval Air Station teaching 50-cal machine gun training for future aerial gunners. He transferred to the US Navy auxiliary air station at Modesto, CA, where he was part of a team effort practicing night carrier landings for cadet pilots.

The war with Japan ended in September 1945. Three months later he was shipped to Ford Island Naval Air Station at Pearl Harbor. Then in early 1946, he was assigned duty aboard the *USS Saratoga*, an aircraft carrier. He served abroad the Saratoga until his discharge from the Navy in June 1946.

Gillen is a graduate of the New York State Institute of Applied Arts and Science in Buffalo NY, class of 1949. He then joined his mentor and future partner, George Wellman professional engineer and land surveyor at Warsaw NY, where they founded the firm of Gillen and Wellman land surveyors. The firm is currently owned by his son John Gillen, Land Surveyor.

Made in the USA
Columbia, SC
05 January 2020